Architectural Guide
Montréal

Architectural Guide
Montréal

Heike Maria Johenning

DOM
publishers

'There is a crack in everything. That is how the light gets in.'

Leonard Cohen

Contents

Montréal with Mont Royal (left in the picture) in winter.

View of the centre of Montréal from Mont Royal.

An island with three mountains

Montréal is a pulsating, sprawling, and green metropolis with an intact historical city centre and a multiplicity of religious buildings and streets designed in European styles and reminiscent of Paris or London. The typical canyons formed by skyscrapers, however, situate the city clearly in North America. The Hochelaga Archipelago, which includes the Île de Montréal, the city's largest island, comprises three lakes, three rivers, 21 rapids, 1000 kilometres of coast, as well as an estimated 325 islands which are connected with the Québec mainland by 30 bridges. The Montréal metropolitan area today has a population of 3.7 million living in an area of 364 square kilometres, of whom approximately 52 per cent are francophones. This multi-ethnic metropolis, as Montréalers call their city, is the fourth largest French-speaking city in the world – after Paris, Kinshasa, and Abidjan. In 2017 the second oldest city on the American continent (after Québec) celebrated its 375th anniversary; in the same year Canada celebrated its 150th. This curious fact has its explanation in chequered Franco-British colonial history. Canada still belongs to the Commonwealth of Nations, an association of former colonies of the British Crown.

View of the centre of Montréal from the east.

View of the islands of Sainte-Hélène (foreground) and Notre-Dame in the St Lawrence River.

A Overview map

Sainte-Anne-
des-Plaines

Blainville

Aéroport International
Montréal-Mirabel

Laval

Pointe-Calumet

Aéroport
Montréal-Trudeau

Lac des Deux-
Montagnes

Lac Saint-
Louis

Île Perrot

Châteauguay

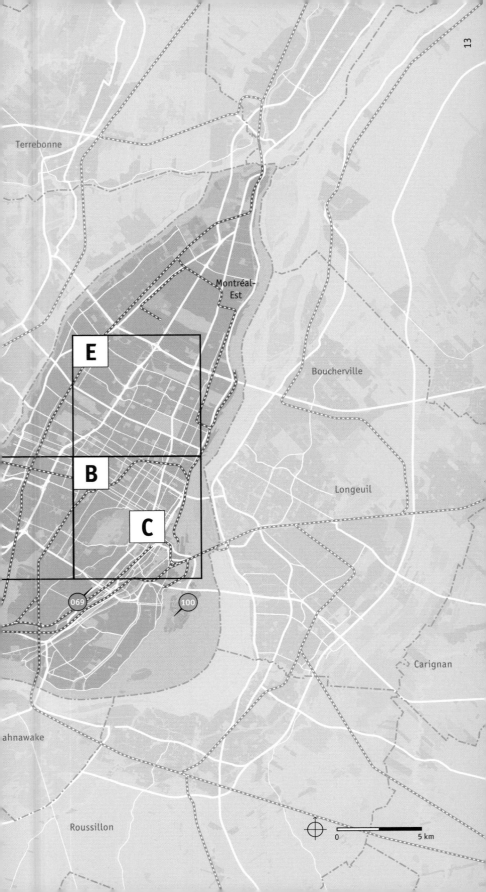

Terrebonne

Montréal–Est

Boucherville

Longeuil

Carignan

ahnawake

Roussillon

E

B

C

069

100

0   5 km

Vieux-Montréal

Colonial architecture since the city's foundation in 1642

Colonial architecture

The Iroquois and Algonquin tribes had been living in the area of the Île de Montréal as far back as 1000 BC. In 1535 the French seafarer Jacques Cartier 'discovered' the 233-metre-high chain of hills on the island in the St Lawrence River and called it 'Mont Royal' ('Royal Mountain') in honour of the then king of France, François I. What is today the city centre of Montréal, however, goes back to the settlement of Ville Marie, which was only founded approximately 100 years later, in 1642, by colonists under a French officer called Paul Chomedey de Maisonneuve and a nun by the name of Jeanne Mance.

Until 1842 it was mainly dwellings and forts that were built to provide security from raids and excessive cold and heat. In 1663 Louis XIV placed the Île de Montréal directly under the French crown; the rights of possession passed to the Sulpician Order. The latter promoted agriculture and built mainly churches. In the following years the Iroquois were pushed out of the settlement, which became a centre for trading in furs. The skins – mostly, beaver furs – were transported through France to Europe by the Hudson's Bay Company, founded in 1670 by two Englishmen in the northern region of Manitoba.
In 1701 the Great Peace of Montréal brought a reconciliation with the indigenous inhabitants of the region.

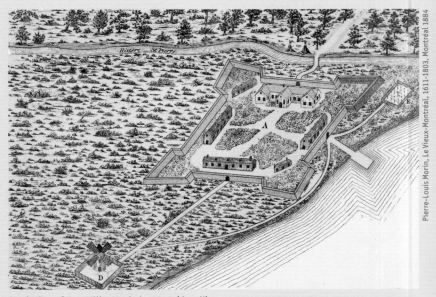

Pierre-Louis Morin, Le Vieux-Montréal, 1611-1803, Montréal 1884

Depiction of Fort Ville-Marie in 1645 (detail).

Gabled brick houses from the nineteenth century.

The village of Ville-Marie, founded in 1642 by the Société Notre-Dame de Montréal.

Meanwhile, the settlers were adapting only slowly due to the difficult climatic conditions. The wooden buildings were difficult to heat; drifts of snow slid unchecked from the roofs. There was a lack of the right instruments to work the limestone, and there were too few craftsmen. Mortar and plaster were relied upon to prevent water penetrating the buildings. Glass was transported from France in the form of small panes of crown glass; large panes were too delicate for the long journey. In 1727 fire walls were required by law. Henceforth, they protruded, like chimneys, far beyond the ridges of the houses' roofs (see: 003).

As a consequence of the growth of British influence in North America, between 1717 and 1738 the French settlers built city walls. After the conquest of Québec and Montréal by Britain in 1763 and an ultimately failed invasion by the American Continental Army (1775/1776), French influence in the British colony of Canada went into steady decline. At this point Montréal had a population of 5200.

From 1800 forwards, the city's wooden structures were replaced with buildings made from local limestone, predominantly in the French manner. The colour of the limestone – a light grey – was to dominate the cityscape for almost 150 years. With the dismantling of the city walls in 1801, Montréal was unleashed, quickly transforming into a large city. The influence of the Roman Catholic Church remained undiminished, as is still evidenced today by countless churches and monasteries from that time. From 1800 forwards, Greek and Roman columns, pediments, domes, and porticos started to appear in the cityscape: British-Scottish architects preferred Classicism; the French style retreated into the background.

Historicism and technological progress between 1824 and 1890

Historicism

A new epoch was heralded by the erection of Notre-Dame Basilica in 1824–1829 in the Historicist style (see: 006). Architects based their design on images from books and on photographs from old Europe. Styles that dominated in Europe, such as Neo-Gothic and Neo-Renaissance, were regarded as worthy of imitation because they stood for tradition, durability, and prosperity. Both styles were developed further and adapted in Montréal. Almost all church buildings from this time are recognisable by Neo-Gothic elements such as pointed arches, pinnacles, and rose windows. The Italian Renaissance style of the fifteenth and sixteenth centuries also experienced a revival, for the most part reaching Montréal by way of England. Distinguished by strong ornamentation, striking cornices, window gables over arched windows, and a Classical façade arrangement, Neo-Renaissance forced the colonial style into retreat and embodied a new prosperity; it became the style of choice for trading houses, banks, and private villas. Additionally, some churches were built based on prototypes in Rome.

The inauguration of the Canal de Lachine in 1825 made it possible for ships to bypass the difficult rapids of the Saint Lawrence River. The city's population grew to 26,000 as a wave of migration from Scotland and Ireland brought new labour resources to the aspiring metropolis. The suburbs were incorporated into the city and linked to the old centre by a grid-like network of streets.

Warehouses and factories were built on either side of the canal; in their construction bricks were used for the first time. Large steel beams and flat roofs made it easier to enclose extensive floor areas. Blind arcades on the façade were often the sole decoration.

Victorian style

Technical progress during the rule of Queen Victoria of Britain (1837–1901) brought the so-called 'Victorian style' to the St Lawrence River too. Essentially, this was a marriage of stylistic elements from the Neo-Gothic and Neo-Renaissance styles: ornamentation, turrets, arched windows, and rusticated socle storeys were intended to convey the idea of financial growth and prosperity.

In 1844–1849 Montréal was the capital of the United Province of Canada, a union of the British colonies of Upper and Lower Canada (until 1869). After riots following attempts at independence, Toronto was for a short time appointed the capital; it was followed by Québec and Ottawa.

From 1850 the city's development accelerated through the introduction of new construction technologies. Urbanisation proceeded apace. It was mainly hotels, shops, and warehouses that were built, but canals and parks were also created. Here we see the first signs of the rationalist style used on the East Coast of America. Many of the commercial buildings that appeared at this time with their simple stone façades and large display windows are to be seen in the old city centre to this day. The first, horse-drawn, trams appeared

Grain silos on the Lachine Canal at dusk.

Nicolas McComber/iStock

Mount Royal Chalet, on the summit of Mount Royal.

in the cityscape. Montréalers' favourite means of transport was, however, the railway – as is clear from the fact that the city has three railway stations. In 1852 a large fire destroyed much of the existing city. At the same time, Neoclassicism disappeared from the architect's repertoire, making room for more modern styles: from Paris came mansard roofs, towers and turrets, and segmental arched windows – appropriate dress for banks and commercial buildings.

The first 'Golden Age'

1867 marked the beginning of Montréal's so-called 'Golden Age'. The construction of the Canadian Pacific Railway linking the Atlantic with the Pacific, the completion of Pont Victoria (Victoria Bridge), and the expansion of the port brought new prosperity to the city. Montréal became the financial centre of the British-dominated North American colony; rue Saint-Jacques, the city's 'Wall Street', was its heart. Grand Victorian buildings replaced the Neoclassical houses. 1867

was also the year when the four provinces of Ontario, Québec, New Brunswick, and Nova Scotia merged to form the Dominion of Canada. The anglophone bourgeoisie now dominated the francophone middle and lower classes as this traditional agrarian country developed into an industrial nation. The first grain silos appeared along the railway line, and in 1883 wheat was for the first time shipped through Montréal's port to Europe. At the foot of Mont Royal private villas, clubs, and expensive hotels sprang up in the part of the city which is still to this day known as the 'Golden Square Mile' with the Musée des Beaux-Arts (see: 052) as its centre. 1876 saw the opening of Mont Royal Park, modelled on Central Park in New York. The Neo-Romanesque style brought façade decoration such as arcades of windows, corner towers, arches, and rows of pilasters and columns (as may be seen on the Gare Windsor and the Erskine and American Church). The castle style (the most important example of which is Le Château; see: 067) emerged from a marriage of French and Scottish architecture.

Late-nineteenth-century commercial buildings in the historical centre of Montréal.

Vieux Séminaire
de Saint-Sulpice
116, rue Notre-Dame Ouest
François Dollier de Casson
1684–1687

001 C

When what is today the oldest building in the city was erected by the Sulpician Order, which had moved from Paris to the Île de Montréal in order to train priests, only approximately 500 people lived in the settlement. The grey, undressed blocks of stone came from a nearby quarry and played a decisive role in shaping the settlement's look at a time when wooden buildings were no longer appropriate. The impressive tower clock (1701) over the entrance was a gift from the French king Louis XIV. The cour d'honneur was the result of alterations carried out in 1705 under the supervision of the superior, François Vachon de Belmont. When in 1840 the Sulpicians' rule over the Île de Montréal came to an end, the school for priests was moved to a new seminary, the Grand Séminaire. The old seminary was supposed to be razed to the ground. In 1852, however, an east wing was built on; the order decided to preserve the ensemble. In 1908 an annex was completed at the rear. The seventeenth-century Baroque garden is today the only one of its kind in North America.

Philipp Meuser

Château Ramezay

280, rue Notre-Dame Est
Architect unknown
1755–1757

002 C

This opulent stone building was originally built as a residence for Claude de Ramezay, the then governor of Québec. In 1745 the house was enlarged and converted for use as a warehouse for furs for the French West Indian Company. In 1754 a fire destroyed large parts of the building; it was rebuilt on the original foundations and extended in the period to 1757. After New France was conquered by the British in 1758–1760, the American revolutionary guard was housed here. In 1775 the Continental Army invaded Québec; Benjamin Franklin spent ten days in the house, along with a contingent of US diplomats, in an attempt to obtain Canadians' support for the American revolution. After this unsuccessful mission,

the three-storey château with its gabled roof became the official residence of the British governor. The interior is impressive: the Salle de Nantes with its grand row of mirrors is now decorated with Louis XV panels which were exhibited as an export product in the French Pavilion at Expo 67. After the last governor moved out in 1844, the building served variously as a courthouse, a primary school, a governmental building, and then as home to the medical and law faculties of Université Laval. In 1903 a tower was added – supposedly to impart a château-like character to the simple grey house with its crown-glass windows (typical for the time of construction: they were easier to transport from Europe). Since 1895 the semi-basement floor – unusually spacious for a Montréal mansion – the vaulted socle storey, and garden in the French style have housed a museum of ethnography and history.

Pgiam/iStock

Heike Maria Johenning

Heike Maria Johenning

Maison Pierre du Calvet
401, rue Bonsecours
Architect unknown
1770

003 C

It is primarily the thick, towering fire wall which makes this three-storey, typically French stone building with its panes of crown glass so distinctive. The disastrous fires that were frequent at that time often leapt onto neighbouring buildings, so fire walls were prescribed by law from 1727 forwards. This large corner building was erected on the foundations of a house built in 1725. The Huguenot merchant Pierre du Calvet lived here until 1780, when he was arrested by the British for advocating the union of Canada with the United States. After his death at sea in 1786, the house was used for various commercial purposes – as an inn, a grocery shop, and even a barber's shop. After a renovation carried out in 1966, the residential building with its preserved original interior was converted for use as exhibition space for the Musée des Beaux-Arts (see: 052). It currently houses a restaurant.

Pgiam/iStock

Chapelle Notre-Dame-de-Bon-Secours

004 C

400, rue Saint-Paul Est
Architect unknown
1771

This place of worship is one of the oldest churches in Montréal. It was built in 1771 on the foundations of a seafarers' chapel at the behest of the nun Marguerite Bourgeoys. A colossal statue of the Virgin Mary as queen of the seas holding up her arms in greeting towards the port has since 1849 adorned the octagonal accessible drum at the back of this Neo-Gothic religious building. This part of the church, subsequently fitted with a veranda, also contains a museum in honour of Marguerite Bourgeoys, a teacher who in 1658 established the congregation of Notre Dame de Montréal, the first female congregation in Canada. Two small towers flank the main entrance, which has a steeple and a small portico. The lead-glass windows let abundant light into the interior, which is decorated with historical models of ships.

1

Heike Maria Johenning

Heike María Johenning

Maison Papineau
440, rue de Bonsecours
Jean-Baptiste Cérat
1785

`005` C

Towards the end of the eighteenth century there were hardly any well-trained craftsmen in Montréal and no instruments suitable for working stone for use in construction. Apart from the basilica of Notre-Dame, this pretty house with its double row of dormer windows is the only building of its time to have a regular façade. However, what we see here is not dressed stone but stone and brick clad with painted wood. Neoclassical with a segmental arched door, this house stands out from the typical grey stone buildings nearby. Its inhabitants have included the well-known politician and lawyer Louis-Joseph Papineau, who led the French-Canadian nationalist movement during the revolution of 1837. After briefly being used as a hotel, this historically important building was bought by the journalist Eric McLean in 1962. He restored it with due regard for its status as a monument and then lived here himself. Since 1982 the house has been in the possession of the Canadian Ministry for the Environment.

Basilique Notre-Dame
116, rue Notre-Dame Ouest
James O'Donnell
1824–1829

`006` C

This is a masterpiece of the Neo-Gothic style in North America, even if the authentic exterior conceals a typical religious building from the time of the industrial revolution. James O'Donnell, its Protestant architect, an Irishman living in New York, was so enamoured of the completed basilica that he converted to Catholicism and had himself buried in the crypt. He had been hired by the Sulpician Order in a bid to provoke the Anglican Church and check its influence in Québec. The Basilique Notre-Dame is very similar to Notre-Dame Cathedral in Paris, but also has a certain resemblance to the Church of St Sulpice in the same city. The rectangular floor plan has a long nave. Above it two 66-metre-high square towers, called 'Tempérance' and 'Persévérance', rise at the front on either side of an arcade of lancet arches above the entrance. The few identically sized bifora windows with lancet arches give this magnificent building a harmonious beauty but admit little light into the interior. For this reason additional

windows were installed in the nave in 1929. Eleven bells made in London fill the two bell-towers, topped by Gothic pinnacles; these have a unique peal which can be heard up to 30 kilometres outside the city. The front façade above the arcade is decorated with blind arches housing sculptures. At the top a row of small battlements serves as the cornice. The outstanding, mystically polychromatic interior derives from the years 1874 to 1880 and is the work of the well-known ecclesiastical architect Victor Bourgeau. Bourgeau and the artist Henri Bouriché opted for wooden fittings with hand-carved finishings and struts painted and/or decorated with gold leaf. The altar, carved from lime and walnut wood, goes especially well with the night-blue ceiling and the likewise blue walls. The imposing ceiling vaulting is decorated with stars made with 24-carat gold. In addition to the organ with its almost 7000 pipes, especially worth seeing are the baptistry and the stained-glass windows by Francis Chigot. A light show in the baptistry tells the church's history every evening. The more intimate chapel of Notre-Dame du Sacré-Cœur in the rear part of the cathedral was added in 1888 but was almost entirely destroyed by a fire in 1978. Only the staircases and the side pews survived. The light-flooded vaulting was built anew with simple wooden furnishings and completed in 1982. It now forms the backdrop to an enormous altarpiece consisting of 32 bronze panels designed by the Montréal artist Charles Daudelin. Here marrying couples daily take their vows. The Basilique Notre-Dame was given the status of *Basilica minor* by Pope John Paul II in 1982.

S. Greg Panosian/iStock

Ancienne-Douane

150, rue Saint-Paul Ouest
John Ostell
1836

007 C

The London-born architect John Ostell (1813–1892) was the best-known architect working in the Neoclassical style in Montréal. This customs house, his first major commission, was his opportunity to show what he could do. Here he created the Montréal archetype of a Neoclassical building, including rusticated socle storey and portico with paired columns and a triangular pediment. The Ancienne-Douane has been part of the Pointe-à-Callière Museum of Archaeology and History, with which it is connected underground, since 1992. Ostell bequeathed the city several other similar imposing buildings, including the Grand Séminaire and the Court of Arbitration in Rue Notre-Dame.

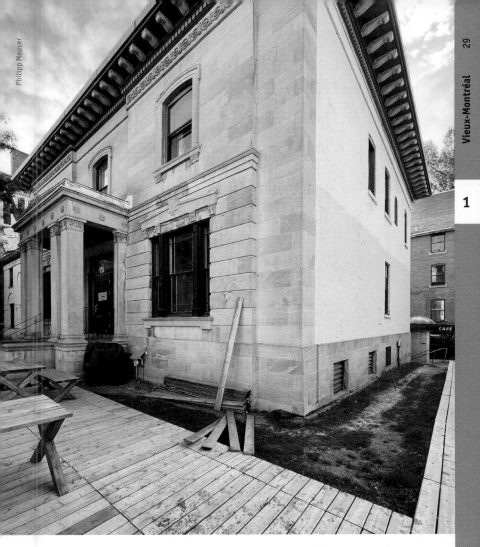

Maison Notman

008 C

51, rue Sherbrooke Ouest
John Wells
1844

At the noisy intersection of rue Peel and avenue des Pins stands this house with its elegant Greek decoration and Doric entrance portico. It was commissioned by William Collis Meredith, the supreme judge at the supreme court of the province of Québec. Untypical for its period, which was dominated by Neoclassicism, this building is a good example of the transition to the Neo-Renaissance style. The grand interior has survived almost entirely intact. Today this urban villa bears the name of its most eminent owner, the photographer William Notman (1826–1891),

who lived here from 1876 to his death. His extensive archive of approximately 400,000 photographs, mostly of daily life in Montréal and the surrounding countryside, is at the Musée McCord and is currently being digitalised.

Bank of Montréal
119, rue Saint-Jacques
John Wells
(interior: McKim,
Mead & White, New York, 1904)
1847

009 C

This veritable temple of Mammon on the place d'Armes was designed by the architect John Wells, who emigrated to Montréal from England in 1830. The inspiration for its design was the headquarters of the Commercial Bank of Scotland in Edinburgh. Canada's oldest bank has resided in this grand Romanesque Revival building since 1847. Reminiscent of the Pantheon in Rome, it has a six-columned portico and a large flat dome, which had to be replaced in 1903. The elaborate bas-relief decorating the pediment was made in Scotland by the sculptor John Steell and brought to Canada by ship. Although not exactly small, the building was extended by the American architect Stanford White in 1901–1905; as part of this project, 32 marble columns and a 20-metre-high coffered ceiling were installed in the banking hall. The Corinthian tops of the exterior columns had to be replaced with aluminium copies in 1970 due to weather damage. A small museum here gives insight into the early days of banking in Canada.

cagkansayin/iStock

Nicolas Mc Comber/iStock

Marché Bonsecours
300, rue Saint-Paul Est
William Footner
1845–1852

010 C

This symmetrical, Palladian-like, block of grey limestone, 163 metres long, with a tin-clad dome resting on a drum and with porticos at the front and back was possibly intended as an appropriate seat for the country's parliament (Montréal became capital of the United Province of Canada in 1840 but lost this status in 1849). It was never used as such, however. It served first as an especially imposing market hall. Then in 1850 the architect George Brown was commissioned to redesign the south part of the building for use as a city hall. Extended with a concert hall, the Neo-Greek ensemble in a prime waterfront location was for a time Montréal's cultural and administrative centre. Doric iron columns specially delivered from England decorate the two sides of the entrance. The market ceased operating in 1961. Despite extensive renovation in the 1960s and a new dome erected in 1978, the city administration continued to use a part of the premises. In 1992, to mark Montréal's 350th anniversary, the building ceremonially reopened as a shopping, restaurant, and exhibition complex. It remains a monumental landmark in the harbour area.

Philipp Meuser

Philipp Meuser

Old Harbour Commissioners' Building

011 C

360, place Royale
Architect unknown
1853

This elongated four-storey corner building housed the quarters of the harbour master when the old harbour (Vieux Port) was still in use and only a stone's throw away. It is a good example of the transition from Neoclassicism to Neo-Renaissance, a process which began in Montréal around 1850. A striking feature is the curved corner, common in commercial buildings of its time. Typical Neoclassical elements are the rusticated socle storey and the order of the façade pilasters. Reminiscences of the Italian Renaissance, on the other hand, are the second-storey aedicula windows (windows framed by columns supporting an entablature and pediment) and the arched windows of the attic storey, which tops a mighty cornice.

Saint-Enfant-Jésus

012 B

5037, rue Saint-Dominique
Victor Bourgeau; Joseph Venne (façade)
1857–1858; 1898 (façade)

This impressive Catholic church at Parc Lahaie dominates the city's Mile End district to this day. Built by the well-known architect Victor Bourgeau in 1857–1858, it was initially a simple chapel erected in the Italian Renaissance style in open countryside, far from the centre of any village. The wedding-cake-like sculptural façade was added only at the end of the nineteenth century. The design of the exterior envelope by a team of architects under Joseph Venne is particularly original. Stylistically, the building would best be classified as Eclectic – a term which denotes the mixing and/or ideally further development of various European architectural styles cited in one and the same building. Supported by a drum, the bell-tower tapers like a pyramid. The bell-tower's basis is a colonnade with six Corinthian columns; the three storeys above it are slightly set back. The church has arched windows and is extravagantly decorated with obelisks, balustrades, cornices, pilasters, and even a polygonal tower superstructure and lantern designed mainly in the Baroque style. In 1908, to mark the church's fiftieth anniversary, two three-metre-high wooden sculptures of angels by the sculptor Joseph-Olindo Gratton were added to the façade. Completed only in 1919, the interior is decorated with dome frescoes by Ozias Leduc (1864–1955), one of the most important Québec painters of his time. Leduc is also the author of scenes in the chapel of the Sacré-Coeur depicting farmers and quarry workers from Saint-Louis-du-Mile-End, the village from which this district of Montréal developed.

Philipp Meuser

Christz Church Cathedral

635, rue Sainte-Catherine Ouest
Frank Wills,
Thomas Seaton Scott
1857–1860

Surrounded by skyscrapers, the Anglican Christ Church Cathedral looks like a Neo-Gothic trompe-l'oeil. Its architect, Frank Wills, brought this style with him from his English home city of Salisbury, where the cathedral has a similar spire. For the façade with its gables, turrets, gargoyles, and a portico consisting of an arcade of lanceted arches, Wills used sandstone specially imported from Caen in France, the motherland of Gothic cathedrals. In contrast with the local grey limestone, the Caen stone was especially suited to the execution of fine ornamentation. Regrettably, the façade has suffered over the course of the years: the relatively soft Caen sandstone is not very weather-resistant. Use was also made here of blocks of dressed local stone, a constant in Montréal's architecture for almost 50 years. The rose window with panes of stained glass came from the London workshops of William Morris and was

transported to Montréal by ship. Because Frank Wills died even before construction work began, his colleague and fellow-Englishman Thomas Seaton Scott took over supervision of the work. The original tower had to be demolished for structural reasons in 1927 because it was leaning more than a metre to the south and the entire nave was in danger of sinking. In 1941 donations made it possible to add a new tower with a lighter aluminium structure. When in 1987 the almost-150-metre-high Tour KPMG was planned for a site behind the cathedral (the church tower is today reflected in the KPGM Tower), the project involved building a parking garage and a shopping centre beneath the cathedral. These bold proposals required a new foundation to support the weight of the church. Thirty-three cylindrical steel piles (caissons) were driven into the rock, including ten from the crypt. Prestressed reinforced-concrete beams were then placed upon the caissons. Today you reach the Promenades Cathédrale by escalators and from there proceed to Underground City (RÉSO). An impressive feature of the simple church interior is the first-class organ, which was made in Québec.

Philipp Meuser

Maison Ravenscrag

1025, avenue des Pins Ouest
John William Hopkins,
William Speirs, Victor Roy
1861–1864

014 B

Perched high up on Mont Royal, this Tuscan-style country house has 72 rooms, an entrance portico, and an imposing driveway. The Renaissance style deriving from Italy was held in high esteem by the British in the nineteenth century, above all by the upper class and their architects. The villa of Sir Hugh Allan is one of the finest buildings in this style in Canada and was at the time of its construction the largest private dwelling in the country. Sir Hugh Allan was a banker, shipowner, and railway magnate who had been born in Scotland; when he died in 1882, he was the richest man in Canada. He named his villa, situated two kilometres from the historical city centre, after his favourite childhood playground: Ravenscraig Castle in East Ayrshire in Scotland. From its square central tower he would watch through his telescope the weekly Allan Line steamer arriving from Glasgow. Maison Ravenscrag is asymmetrical with bay windows, columns, balconies, and bifora windows; a surprising element is the pediment in its left half. The grey local limestone has been worked with particular care. As you would expect in a dwelling of this class, it was fitted with state-of-the-art technology, including gas lighting and the most sophisticated heating system of the day. Its grounds occupy an area of five hectares on the edge of the Golden Square Mile, Montréal's most prosperous district. Sir Hugh Allan's illustrious guests included politicians and members of royalty. At the end of World War II the villa was donated by Hugh Allan's son, Montagu Allan, for use by the Hôpital Royal Victoria's Psychiatric Clinic (the Allan Memorial Institute; see: 034). The opulent wooden veranda on the garden side, the balustrades topping the tower, and the ballroom decorated with chandeliers and period furniture were almost completely removed. The greenhouse and the stables also disappeared. Parts of the library and the carved mermaids decorating the walls have been preserved. The mainly Victorian interior with its frescoes no longer exists. For years the city's administration has been working to have this valuable piece of heritage transferred to the Mont Royal Fund prior to full restoration.

Église du Gesù

1202, rue de Bleury
Patrick C. Keely
1865

An external staircase leads visitors through one of the three arched portals into this Jesuit church faced with undressed stone. The Jesuits hired an architect from Brooklyn to design a building in the Neo-Renaissance style that would do justice to the resilience of their order, which had been dissolved in 1773 and then reconstituted by Pius VII in 1814. Bishop Ignace Bourget asked Patrick C. Keely, who had at that time already built 100 churches, to create a façade resembling the Baroque Church of Il Gesù in Rome, which houses the tomb of St Ignatius of Loyola, the society's founder. Keely, however, designed a kind of Italian palazzo with a hipped roof, albeit with a cruciform ground plan. The four-storey building has over the course of the years been hemmed in by high-rises, with the result that the front side, which is decorated with arched windows, can only be seen properly from close up. On either side of the entrance stands a three-storey square tower, slightly set back. The towers were supposed to be topped by domes, but the original design remained unrealised for reasons of cost. In 1976 the order's management decided to have the adjacent Jesuit College demolished. The Église du Gesù, in which Canada's first electric candlelight shone in 1878, was preserved. It temporarily housed one of the city's oldest theatres until it was renovated in the 1980s.

Philipp Meuser

Philipp Meuser

Molson Bank

288, rue Saint-Jacques
George Brown
1866

016 C

The Molson brewery dynasty possessed what was almost a license to print money in Montréal. Its founder, John Molson (1763–1836), immigrated from Lincolnshire and was subsequently successful dealing in real estate. He also played a part in financing the construction of railways, built Canada's first steamship, and established the St Lawrence Steamboat Company, which had a fleet of ships larger than the entire combined fleet of the United States. His descendants William and John jr. founded their own bank in 1853 (bought by the Bank of Montreal in 1925). This grand three-storey palace completed in 1866 with its columned portico, rusticated socle storey, and sophisticated segmental windows gives little clue that it is in

fact a bank. Despite the undefinable roof construction, which resembles a mansard roof, the building looks very French. The façade is extremely plastic: the front side is decorated with Corinthian pilasters and columns, consoles, cartouches, floral ornamentation, and an attic over the central portico with its balcony. As a reminder of the family's forbears, portraits of Thomas Molson (1791–1863), a co-founder of the brewery, and his children were engraved in place of keystones or mascarons in the polished sandstone above the windows on the raised ground floor. In the 1930s St James Street – today: rue St Jacques – was Canada's Wall Street. Situated near the Pont Jacques Cartier, the Molson family's brewery building has a unique tower clock and is North America's oldest brewery but is soon to be replaced with a new building in the suburb of Longueuil. It is not yet clear what is to be the fate of the historical factory complex on the Saint Lawrence River.

St. Paul
3415, Redpath Street;
615, av. Sainte-Croix
Lawford & Nelson
1867

017 D

In the nineteenth century it was primarily Scottish immigrants who determined Canada's economic fate. The Scottish parish of St Paul's was founded in 1832. To demonstrate its influence, in 1867 the community had an Anglo-Saxon-Presbyterian church built in the city centre, on what was then Dorchester Boulevard (today: boulevard René-Lévesque). The city church built by Frederick Lawford, an architect who had trained in London, and his Canadian colleague James Nelson served as the seat of four powerful groups or clans of Presbyterians. When it was decided in 1927 to build the main railway station (see: 091), the church was slated for demolition. The Catholic congregation of the Holy Cross in France bought the building for a symbolic dollar and had it reassembled on another site without further ado. In only 60 days the church was dismantled, stone by stone, and rebuilt on land belonging to Saint-Lawrence College 15 kilometres to the west. The rebuilding of this Neo-Gothic ensemble with its square clock tower and annexes with pointed gables was overseen by the architect Lucien Parent. Parent slightly changed the design because the church was now to be used as a Catholic place of worship. Additionally, the building was raised by one storey to accommodate the Salle Émile-Legault, home to a theatre company specialising in French-speaking productions, on the ground floor. In 1979 the church was converted into a museum for traditional crafts and is now known as the Musée des maîtres et artisans du Québec.

Magasin-entrepôt Récollet
457, rue Sainte-Hélène
Cyrus P. Thomas
1868

018 C

This building in the centre of Vieux-Montréal was designed by Cyrus P. Thomas, a member of a Toronto family of architects, as a department store selling dry goods. The land had belonged to a Franciscan community called Les Récollets, but the latter had had to sell the plot. The original building was four storeys high with an expressively jutting cornice, a curved corner, and large, inviting arched windows. A fifth storey topped by a series of string courses and a much simpler cornice was added in 1906. This part of the old city contains the largest ensemble of buildings in the Neo-Renaissance style in Montréal. Almost all these edifices, which are faced with high-quality sandstone, have been renovated in recent decades and now once again house shops, restaurants, or hotels.

Philipp Meuser

Hôtel Gault
449, rue Sainte-Hélène
John James Browne
1871

019 C

Carpets, furniture, and fabrics from all over the world were once sold in this former department store. The five-storey building with one curved corner fits harmoniously into the development in the old city and is one of several commercial buildings which were designed in the Second Empire style and not, as was usual at that time, in that of the Neo-Renaissance. Large segmental arched windows and doors, cartouches above the windows, and an austere order of pilasters give this corner building a distinctive, very French, appearance. The plastic façade is horizontally emphasised by two cornices, of which the cornice above the fourth storey is especially emphatic. The large rooms with high ceilings are perfect for the boutique hotel which its present owner, the tech guru and special effects producer Daniel Langlois, opened here in 2002 after having the building extensively renovated.

Cathédrale Marie-Reine-du-Monde

1085, rue de la Cathédrale

Victor Bourgeau,
Joseph Michaud

1870–1894

020 C

At the time of its construction it must have been somewhat of a surprise to come across this cathedral, a kind of reduced-size version of St Peter's in Rome, on the corner of René Lévesque Boulevard and Metcalfe Street, in the heart of Montréal's English community. The reasons for its presence here have primarily to do with relations between religions. The then bishop of Montréal, Ignace Bourget, wanted to turn the city into the main stronghold of the Roman Catholic Church in North America, in the midst of a Protestant majority. Protestant churches were at this time mostly in the Neo-Gothic style, so Neo-Renaissance was chosen as the dominant style here. The grandiose church was consecrated to the Virgin Mary; the emotive addition 'Queen of the World' conveyed an important message. Victor Bourgeau, the church's architect, was specially sent to Rome in 1859 to study St Peter's. In 1878, however, the money ran out, so the church with its opulent dome (diameter: 23 metres) ended up only a third of the size of its Roman prototype. In the severe Canadian winters this small building was, however, easier to heat. When Victor Bourgeau died in 1888, the chaplain, Joseph Michaud, took over supervision of the construction work. The 76-metre-high building with its enormous portico stands out for several elements that are typical of Montréal architecture, e.g. the unplastered or dressed grey limestone, the copper roof, and the 13 statues of saints carved from wood and clad with copper (symbolising the 13 parishes of Montréal which paid for the building). The nave with its light-coloured coffered ceiling is relatively simple in style. The altar is a successful copy of the Baroque baldachin by Gian Lorenzo Bernini in St Peter's; this is the work of the Montréal sculptor Joseph-Arthur Vincent. The Montréal archdiocese's unique cathedral was designated a *Basilica minor* by Pope Benedict XV in 1919.

Nicolas McComber/iStock

116 1000 De La Gauchetièr

020 Cathédrale Marie-Reine-du-Monde

Le Château Champlain 093

029 Gare Windsor

Philipp Meuser

BASILIQUE   MARIE-REINE-DU-MONDE   CATHÉDRALE

Maison Shaughnessy
1923, boul.
René-Lévesque Ouest
William Tutin Thomas
1874

The Second Empire style was in full bloom when this three-storey double house with mansard roof, forged-iron roof decoration, and rectangular bay windows stretching over three storeys was built for two clients – a timber trader and a railway magnate. Typical of this French architectural style are the large arched and segmental arched windows with cartouches and the arcaded canopies over the entrances at either side of this mirror-inverted double house. The ground storey is emphasised by being raised above a semi-basement storey. In 1890 the small, circular winter garden with its polygonal dome was added at the west entrance; this is supported by a kind of drum. When the owners wanted to part ways with this urban palace in 1974, it was bought by the architect and philanthropist Phyllis Lambert. She had the ageing building restored by Denis Saint-Louis in 1988 and the interior converted to offices and exhibition spaces. For decades Lambert was curator of the Centre Canadien d'Architecture (CCA; see: 114), which was situated on the same piece of land and to which the ornate villa, listed as a monument since 1973, now belongs. Some of the opulently furnished rooms are for this reason open to the public today.

Philipp Meuser

Heike Maria Johenning

Hôtel de Ville
275, rue Notre-Dame Est
*Henri-Maurice Perrault/
Louis Parant*
1872–1878/1922

022 C

This grandiose five-storeyed limestone building with a two-storey portico and a columned risalite has a tall mansard roof, a clock-tower with a polygonal dome, and a tower-clock. The upper storeys were designed in a brilliant Beaux-Arts style after this part of the building was destroyed in a fire in 1922. The bottom two storeys, where the fire was extinguished in time, still have the original façade in the Neo-Renaissance style. The city's archive also went up in flames in the same fire, making it difficult even today to find historical information on buildings in Montréal. The city's architect Louis Parant was commissioned to reconstruct the building. He placed a self-supporting steel framework inside the shell of the ruins and opted for a steep and tall Beaux-Arts-type mansard roof clad in copper instead of the original panels of slate. He took as his model the city hall building in Tours in France. Pictures of the reconstructed city hall went all round the world when on 24 July 1967 Charles de Gaulle shouted his famous 'Vive le Québec libre!' from its balcony – to the joy of the separatists. Since 2017 a fresh wind has been blowing through the old walls. Montréal now has its first female mayor: Valérie Plante.

Heather Shimmin/iStock

Philipp Meuser

Exchange Bank Building
204, rue Notre-Dame Ouest
John William Hopkins
1874

023 C

The words 'British Empire Building' still stand in bronze-coloured letters above the ground floor of this corner building in the Neo-Renaissance style. It was actually designed as a bank building. The well-known Canadian architect John William Hopkins seems to have based his design, which features all arched windows, on an Italian palazzo with ornamented bifore and Corinthian half-columns. Hopkins thought it important to have an opulent cornice; this was said to be his trademark. The Maison Ravenscrag (see: 014), in whose design he had a hand, also has this feature, which is here reinforced by a series of emphatic string courses between storeys. Not least due to its charming oblique corner housing the main entrance, this former bank building fits harmoniously into the surrounding development in the old city.

Harbour Commissioners' Building

024 C

357, rue de la Commune Ouest
John William Hopkins,
Alexander Hutchison
1874–1876

This building with its enormous polygonal dome and wrought-iron balconies is a kind of landmark in Montréal's Old Port, its dominance underlined by the square tower decorated with arched windows, vases, and pilasters in its central part – a feature which rises like a lighthouse two storeys above the truncated pavilion roof. The fact that the design was worked upon by two architects with directly opposing stylistic preferences – the Second Empire style in one case and the Neo-Renaissance style in the other – makes this eclectic building unique. Elements of the Renaissance style exhibited by the façade include aedicula windows, some of which are framed with half-columns, and the symmetrical placement of the two volumes slightly set back on either side of the tower. The Second Empire style is to be seen in the storey height, which diminishes towards the building's top, and in the Neo-Baroque manner in which the façade is adorned with pilasters and columns. The Harbour Commissioners' Building was restored in 2001 (architects: Fournier, Gersovitz, Moss & Associés). Since then the harbourmaster's office, which once greeted ship's captains from all over the world, has gleamed with a new splendour. Today an exclusive private club operates here. The adjacent two-storey office building with its low octagonal tower superstructure was built in 1858. This was the headquarters of the shipping firm of Hugh Allan, whose ship *Virginian* was in 1912 the first to reach the *Titanic* after the latter's captain had sent out a distress signal. It was Allan's firm too that relayed the news of the *Titanic*'s imminent sinking to the newspaper *The Gazette*.

Philipp Meuser

Heike Maria Johenning

Chapelle
Notre-Dame-de-Lourdes
430, rue Ste-Catherine Est
Napoléon Bourassa,
Adolphe Lévesque
1873–1876

025 B

The style of this religious building, which looks massive and slightly overloaded, may be described as a symbiosis of Neo-Romanesque, Neo-Venetian, and Neo-Byzantine influences. On a rectangular ground plan, behind a heavily ornamented three-storey front structure with bifora windows and a rose window, rises a tall drum supporting a magnificent circular dome and fringed by four small towers. Two wings topped by half-domes turn the 'chapel' into an exceptionally spacious, even 'cathedral-like', place of worship, over whose entrance a gold-leaf-covered sculpture of the Virgin Mary seems to float in the air. The Sulpicians, who were once powerful in Montréal, collected donations for the building and chose an architect who was also active as a painter, decorator, and novelist. Napoléon Bourassa had studied numerous different styles on a trip to Europe and now sought to use them all in this chapel, which he regarded as a 'jewel'. The paintings and frescoes in the already very highly coloured interior, decorated with pictures showing the lives of the Virgin Mary and other biblical figures, are likewise by him. Originally, a towering Neo-Gothic bell-tower in the immediate vicinity belonged to this church complex. Following several fires, however, the bell-tower was incorporated in the new building of the Université du Québec à Montréal (UQAM). Its interior today serves as the cafeteria Pavillon Judith-Jasmine.

Le Mount Stephen Hotel
1440, rue Drummond
William T. Thomas/
Lemay Architects
1880–1883/2015–2019

026 C

This two-storey Neo-Renaissance villa is well known to many Hollywood stars. Built by the businessman George Stephen towards the end of the nineteenth century and regarded as an especially successful example of the architecture of its time, it has been used as the location for various historical films. In 1971 it was even voted one of the best Neo-Renaissance buildings in Canada. Also notable is the palace's rich and artistic ornamentation, which sets it apart from other contemporary buildings in Montréal. The ensemble functioned as the Mount Stephen Club in 1926–2011. Its austere appearance is softened by the fact that the two halves of the building are of different design. On the left a separate one-storey structure with a circular ground plan culminates in a curved bay window. The right side of the building has no bay windows. Six columns support the portico, which is topped with a balcony. The English architect William Tutin Thomas was regarded as one of the best architects of his time; he had been apprenticed to his uncle John Thomas, a well-known sculptor who contributed to the façade of Westminster Palace and to Westminster Palace. Typically Victorian are the borrowings of British and Italian decorative elements, nowhere else in Montréal to be found in such perfection. This makes it the more tragic that when the building was being converted into a boutique hotel with an underground car park in 2016, the façade subsided and cracks appeared in the masonry. The building had to be propped up and then repaired at great expense. The interior, which has been preserved almost in its entirety, is still luxurious by today's standards. For the wooden panelling rare woods, including mahogany from Cuba, walnut from England, and satinwood from Sri Lanka, were shipped to Montréal. Some of the rooms have stained-glass mosaics from Austria and Germany. The client, George Stephen, is regarded as one of the most important bankers in the history of Canada; he was initially president of the Bank of Montreal and later of the Canadian Pacific Railway, receiving the title of baron for his services. His palace is today the nucleus of a luxury hotel whose block-shaped twelve-storey extension with a contrasting pixelated skin in the rear courtyard sets off this architectural jewel to great effect. In the dark the villa appears to be illuminated from behind by window openings of different sizes on a façade of 1000 concrete elements arranged in a diamond grid pattern. This returns it to what it was in its heyday: a Canadian landmark.

Redpath Museum
859, rue Sherbrooke Ouest
A. C. Hutchison and A. D. Steele
1880–1882

027 C

Perched on an eminence on the McGill University campus, the ensemble of buildings of the Redpath Museum (museum of natural history) was commissioned by the well-known natural scientist Sir William Dawson in 1880. Standing on an asymmetrical ground plan, this complex is mainly a marriage of two styles: Victorian Classicism and Neo-Renaissance. The portico with round columns, a pediment, and long narrow windows in the front part of the building is picked up on the side wings by two additional stylised porticos; these have small rectangular columns. Designed to look like a basilica with a set-back, curving attic storey, the museum building flows at its rear into a semi-circular section with rectangular colonnades and large windows that admit an abundance of light into the interior. The building is named after the industrialist Peter Redpath (1821–1894), who in the nineteenth century built Canada's first sugar refinery (still in operation today). Redpath also provided the funding for the construction of the museum and for a library on the same campus. Opened in 1882, the Redpath Museum is Canada's oldest building specifically designed as a museum. Originally, it was intended for the sole use of the university; it was only in 1952 that its collections were opened to the public.

Philipp Meuser

Philipp Meuser

Collège du Mont-Saint-Louis

244, rue Sherbrooke Est
Jean-Zéphirin Resther
1887

Towards the end of the nineteenth century Franco-Canadian institutions and religious buildings were often designed in the Second Empire style. This style was already out of fashion with the Anglo-Saxon elite but was still regarded by the francophone population as typically French and thus as a connection with the motherland, France. In the case of the Collège du Mont-Saint-Louis, a school for boys, the budget was limited, so the only clear reference to the Second Empire style is the mansard roof. The polygonal helmet tower over the risalite in the middle of the building forms the focal point and entrance of the otherwise simple and symmetrical five-storey block. In 1987–1989 the architects Claude Gagnon and Guy Legault modernised this enormous building, converting it into an apartment block with 105 residential units. The most recent phase of the conversion involved excavating the front garden so as to create an underground car park.

Philipp Meuser

Philipp Meuser

Gare Windsor
1100, av. des Canadiens-de-Montréal
Bruce Price
1887–1889

029 C

The Canadian Pacific Railway, Canada's state railway, was founded in 1881. It was not long before it emerged that the Gare Dalhousie, which had opened in 1884, would soon be unable to cope with the constantly growing flows of passengers. At that time American architecture was in fashion, so it was the New York architect Bruce Price who got the contract to build a new railway station, named Gare Windsor (Windsor Station) after the street on which it stood (today: Peel Street). He designed a monumental, castle-like building in the Neo-Romanesque style favoured by the architect Henry Hobson Richardson. This ultimately became the Canadian Pacific's main station and main administrative building as the company expanded its operations, its approximately 5000 kilometres of track stretching over the entire continent to Vancouver. The first locomotives left the imposing five-storey terminal station with its gigantic arched windows in 1889. Richardson had established his own style – 'Neo-Romanesque Richardson style' – in America; it is also to be found in many locations in Montréal.

Philipp Meuser

The block has an asymmetrical ground plan. Its most eye-catching features are the two square towers, which rise to a height of up to seven storeys above the rest of the station complex. The enormous tower in the front part is topped by small pointed gables, giving the station with its façade of unworked sandstone, arcades, corner towers, and triangular gables a fortress-like character. In later years an elaborate canopy was added to the arcades of gables over the main entrance. In 1900 the building was extended; a second extension followed in 1909–1914. After intercity railway traffic was discontinued in 1986, followed by the cessation of all rail operations in 1993,

an ice-hockey stadium (Centre Bell) was built on the tracks leading into the station, in effect severing it at a blow from the railway network. Three years later, in 1996, the railway company (today: VIA Rail Canada) moved its headquarters to Calgary and sold Gare Windsor to a property-management company from Toronto. The new owner now operates a hotel, restaurant, and office complex here; part of the complex continues to be rented to the Canadian railway administration. In 2017 the former station hall with its glass-and-steel roof was converted, becoming the entrance to Underground City (RÉSO). Currently, the station building is undergoing renovation.

New York Life Insurance Building

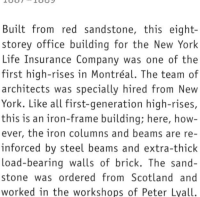

511, place d'Armes
Babb, Cook and Willard
1887–1889

Built from red sandstone, this eight-storey office building for the New York Life Insurance Company was one of the first high-rises in Montréal. The team of architects was specially hired from New York. Like all first-generation high-rises, this is an iron-frame building; here, however, the iron columns and beams are reinforced by steel beams and extra-thick load-bearing walls of brick. The sandstone was ordered from Scotland and worked in the workshops of Peter Lyall. Decorated with Neo-Renaissance elements but no columns, the New York Life Insurance Building is given a vertical emphasis by its square clock tower which, topped by a small lantern and balustrades, rises two storeys above the left part of the building. The ground floor features a two-storey arched portal. The stone ornamentation consisting of arabesques and the mascarons over the third-floor windows came from the atelier of Henry Beaumont. The arch motif is repeated on the sixth to the eighth storeys in the form of an arcade, giving this office building an Italian grandeur. A second stone balustrade tops the roof. The fact that the windows are wider than they are high is an innovation made by the Chicago School and remains a mark of American architecture to this day. The inscription above the building's entrance reads 'The Québec Bank, established 1818'. At the time of its construction the building was fitted with the most advanced equipment of its time, including hydraulic elevators, a fire-fighting system incorporating water reservoirs (housed in the tower), and electricity. The building originally contained an impressively large library of law books, accessible to tenants renting offices here. The current owner of this historically important building is the architecture professor Bechara Helal. In 2007 Helal had two penthouses built slightly set back on the roof. He lives in one of them himself.

Maison James Phymister
344, av. Metcalfe (Westmount)
Architect unknown
1888

031 B

The name of the architect of this two-storey house with two large wooden verandas in the former suburb of Westmount has not come down to us. This is one of the few buildings in Montréal in the so-called 'Queen Anne style'. Popular in Great Britain in the 1870s, the Queen Anne style looked to historical prototypes in Flemish, French, and English Renaissance architecture. Use was also made of late-Gothic elements. The mostly asymmetrical buildings were imaginatively decorated with towers, gables, overhanging eaves, towering chimneys, and spacious porches and had façades clad with bricks, wood, terracotta, and plaster. Montréalers, however, had little liking for this picturesque eclectic style, continuing to prefer the local limestone for its high quality and robust severity. This makes the Maison James Phymister a slightly alien presence amidst the surrounding development.

Heike Maria Johenning

Maison Peter Lyall
1445, rue Bishop
John James Browne
1889

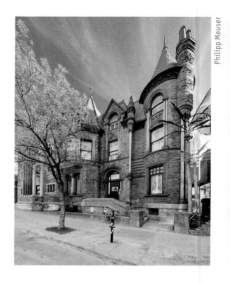

Philipp Meuser

This Victorian private villa stands out for its construction material – red sandstone. This was ballast stone which was loaded onto empty ships coming from Europe so that they could keep to their course when making the long journey. Peter Lyall, who commissioned this house, was himself in the construction business and so had little difficulty in importing this high-quality stone from Scotland. Additionally, the façade design of the asymmetrical two-storey palace with its striking corner tower employed brown sandstone. Their workability makes both types of stone especially suited to this kind of ornamentation. Polychromatic façades were in fashion in the period between 1885 and 1900. The ornamentation came from the atelier of Henry Beaumont, a local artist who had trained in London and Edinburgh. The interior of this house, which is situated in the middle of the Golden Square Mile and is distinguished from the rest of the street by its pointed gables and bay windows, was also elaborately decorated and has been preserved in its original condition.

Vieux Sun Life

268, rue Notre-Dame Ouest
Robert Findlay
1890

The Scottish architect Robert Findlay had many prominent clients in the Golden Square Mile, for whom he built opulent private houses. For the Sun Life Insurance Company he designed an eclectic, mainly Neo-Baroque, six-storey building with curved bay windows and a square corner tower, elaborate loggias, and gables. The sandstone façades are decorated with columns and pilasters, cornices, string courses, and plasterwork. The numerous sculptures are the work of Henry Beaumont. A caryatid replaces one of the columns of the entrance and is the only one of its kind in Vieux-Montréal. In 1908 Sun Life took over the premises of the nearby red-brick Waddell Building. Five years later, the company moved into a gigantic new building on Dorchester Square (see: 054).

Philipp Meuser

The Chicago School and Art Deco

The Chicago School, École des Beaux-Arts, and Art Deco, 1890–1950

From 1883 forwards, many suburbs were incorporated into Montréal. The first theatres and cinemas were built. The Quartier Latin, a district for students named after its prototype in far-away Paris, also dates to this time. New construction materials and a large choice of types of stone injected variation and, above all, colour into Montréal architecture.

After 1890 new architectural styles emerged in the cityscape. The Chicago School brought the first high-rise buildings, made possible by the invention of the elevator. Residential buildings of more than ten storeys with steel skeletons and uniform rows of windows and terracotta and metal cladding as façade decoration also changed the look of Canada's boomtown.

The World's Fair held in Chicago in 1893 brought a new architecture school from Paris to America. The style of the École des Beaux-Arts was based on symmetry and the creation of brightly clad large buildings for institutions, as well as department stores, theatres, and private houses. Balusters, paired columns, caryatids, and filigree iron balcony railings introduced a Parisian flair. Today this period is recalled, for instance, by the First Sun Life Building (see: 033) and the Hotel Ritz-Carlton (see: 050). The Rue Sainte-Catherine was Montréal's most important shopping street. The first buildings in the Art Nouveau style now made their

Art Deco symbol of Québec's first dairy.

appearance in the cityscape. Segmental arches became common as display windows for department stores; rounded corners were made possible by the use of concrete as a construction material; and façades were for the first time clad with beige-coloured tiles. Regrettably, only a few buildings in this style have survived in Montréal today.

Canada's entering the war on the side of Great Britain in 1914 had dramatic consequences for the city. Montréal ran up debts as it organised deliveries of wood, wheat, copper, steel, and airplane parts in

Right: metal staircases on Place St Louis.

Heike Maria Johenning

payment for the stationing of British marines on the East Coast. In 1918 the port of Montréal was the largest exporter of wheat in North America. Grain silos became part of the city's architectural legacy, even if their construction has its roots in engineering from the US. Regarded as 'cathedrals of the new age', the silos acquired iconic value for Canadians. In 1921 Montréal had a population of 620,000, living mainly in two- or three-storey apartment blocks. Because each apartment was supposed to have at least one balcony and ideally its own entrance, a connection to the upper storeys was required. This led to the birth of the distinctive, usually curving Montréal front-garden staircase made from either wood or metal, a feature which continues to fulfil its function to this day. The front-garden staircase made it possible to avoid any loss of living space inside a house (an internal staircase would also have leaked heat up to the second storey). Bay windows, balconies, and loggias began to appear on three-storey standardised apartment blocks.

Pont Jacques-Cartier and a clock-tower in the Art Deco style.

1920 to 1950

From the beginning of the 1920s to the end of the 1930s Montréal's architecture was stirred by new currents brought by Art Deco. The new art of ornamentation concealed behind this stylistic phenomenon came originally from France, where in 1925 it was showcased at the *Exposition Internationale des Arts Décoratifs et Industriels Modernes* (International Exhibition of Modern Decorative and Industrial Arts) in Paris. The term 'Art Deco' became a stylistic designation for the French and international movement in the fields of design, artistic crafts, and visual art. It is little known, however, that Art Deco architecture (in contrast with interior design and decorative arts) developed in North America, not in Europe.

Even the term 'Art Deco architecture' was first coined in the 1960s, several decades after the Paris exhibition. This style, which emphasises verticality, was to become a highly refined architectural style of its own not only in New York and Miami, but also, and above all, in Montréal. The latter is hardly surprising, given the affinity French Canada felt with France, its motherland. Typical features were set-back building volumes, vertical fluting on the façade, bas-reliefs, geometrical and floral patterns, high-quality materials, and the absence of cornices and string courses. The Art Deco style was regarded as the perfect mix of French ornamentation and American innovation. In her book *Northern Deco* Sandra Cohen-Rose writes

that this style 'came earlier to Montréal than most North American cities.' Today there are still more than 60 Art Deco buildings in Montréal. The Pont Jacques-Cartier, for instance, erected in 1930, bore a great resemblance to Brooklyn Bridge in New York. It became a symbol of a new era in which architects looked for inspiration to the US and, above all, to New York.

During World War II Montréal benefitted from its role in production of supplies. Its busy port, coupled with accelerated trade with the USA, helped it grow into a new economic hub on the East Coast. At the *Exposition Internationale des Arts et Techniques dans la Vie Moderne* (International Exhibition of Arts and Techniques in Modern Life) in Paris in

1937 Canada's pavilion took the form of a grain silo with six concrete cylinders.

Architecturally, Modernism's arrival on the scene was marked by horizontal lines and rows of windows, glass blocks, and rounded corners. The relatively low buildings with their aerodynamic forms embodied a Futurism which spread optimism in the post-war years. Fundamentally, Modernism was a development of the Art Deco style. It was not for nothing that it was also known as 'streamline Modernism': buildings designed in this style resemble the dynamic forms of steamships. Most had at least one flagpole; some had railings or porthole windows. Unlike in Europe, in Montréal in particular this style continued to be used until 1959.

Hôpital Royal Victoria

687, avenue des Pins Ouest
Henry Saxon Snell
1891–1894

034 B

The Hôpital Royal Victoria seems to have landed here from another world. The castle-like exteriors of its seven gigantic individual buildings nestling picturesquely on the slope of Mont Royal would hardly lead you to suspect a hospital. The funding for this hospital complex, extremely well-equipped and expensive for its time, came from Lord Mount Stephen and Lord Strathcona, both of whom had made their fortunes as railway entrepreneurs. The main building of the Hôpital Royal Victoria (later known as the 'Royal Vic') is a transverse block, seven storeys high in the middle, with a three-storey loggia, several stepped gables, a tower, and a cour d'honneur. Small towers soaring at the corners emphasise verticality. On either side of the middle section are two longer sections in the form of risalites; each of these is fronted by two fortress-like, five-storey corner towers. Cast-iron verandas were installed between the towers at a later date. The English-born architect Henry Saxon Snell had already designed other clinics. Here too he chose a U-shaped ground plan. The façade is of traditional grey Montréal limestone. Stylistically, this building resembles the Royal Edinburgh Hospital; the Scottish feel is reinforced by the conical slate roofs, small roof dormers, stepped gables, and pointed towers. Two further annexes stretch behind the main building and differ stylistically only in each having a large pointed gable and a square observation tower. The loggias on

Heike Maria Johenning

each storey, some of which are three storeys high, were also an innovation. The Pavillon Hersey, completed in 1905, was designed by the well-known local architects Edward and William Sutherland Maxwell and housed Canada's first nursing school. In the area lying between the pavilion and Maison Ravenscrag (Allan Memorial Institute; see: 014), there was even a pool. In 1920 the Hôpital Royal Victoria became the university clinic of McGill University and thus a teaching hospital. 1934 brought the opening of the Montréal Neurological Institute, today regarded as one of the best institutions of its kind in the world. In the second half of the twentieth century an undecorated dormitory tower was added to the ensemble. In 2015 a large part of the hospital moved to a new building in a suburb of Montréal, where it operates as 'the Glen Clinic'. Only the maternity centre and the dialysis clinic have remained on the campus, whose future now seems secure. McGill University plans to renovate the historical buildings and build an extension equipped with a geothermal system as a new research centre. This will, however, necessitate the demolition of two pavilions behind the main building. The new extension will be of a lower height, opening up again views of Mont Royal from the original buildings. The car park in front of the old hospital will be turned back into a green courtyard, in keeping with the plans for this site devised by Frederick Law Olmsted in 1877. Two large classrooms and an events space with four skylights permitting views of the heritage buildings above will be built under the courtyard. The 'New Vic' should be ready in 2028.

Philipp Meuser

Monument-National
(Centre culturel de Société
Saint-Jean-Baptiste)
1182, boul. Saint-Laurent
Maurice Perrault, Albert Mesnard
and Joseph Venne
1891–1893

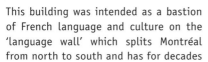

035 C

This building was intended as a bastion of French language and culture on the 'language wall' which splits Montréal from north to south and has for decades divided the city into English- and French-speaking districts (even today, in fact, the Boulevard Saint Laurent offers a journey back in time to Montréal's bilingual roots). This majestic four-storey building contained a plethora of spaces in which francophones could feel secure: not just a 1400-seat theatre but also shops, classrooms, multifunctional spaces, offices, a library, and a museum. The façade is a screen of muscular grey stone pierced with large and variously shaped expanses of glass. Here Neo-Romanesque borrowings enter into a symbiosis with Neo-Baroque elements. Each storey is of different design but is integrated into an overarching order of pilasters. The ground floor has large rectangular display windows. Above them are arched windows, followed by a row of smaller rectangular windows. The top and tallest storey mixes segmental arched and arched windows. The impression that the flat roof superstructure is incomplete is not deceptive. The two recesses in the cornice are reminders of unrealised exotic lanterns which had to be abandoned for financial reasons.

Philipp Meuser

Erskine and American United Church
1339, rue Sherbrooke Ouest
Alexander Cowper Hutchison
1892

036 C

This imposing church with striking square clock tower was extensively renovated in the period up to 2011. It was originally the church of the city's Presbyterian community (the Erskine Church took its name from Ebenezer and Ralph Erskine, leaders of the Secession Church in Scotland in the eighteenth century; it became the Erskine and American Church when it merged with the American Presbyterian Church in 1934). Following the addition of a new glass annex and a change of name (to Pavillon Claire et Marc Bourgie), it is now an exhibition and concert space belonging to Montréal's Musée des Beaux-Arts (see: 052). A 45-metre-long passage links it to the other museum buildings. Built in the Neo-Romanesque style, the church is asymmetrical with a façade of rusticated limestone, small gables, and rows of windows consisting of long narrow panes, some of which are decorated with columns. The inspiration for the design by the renowned architect Alexander Cowper Hutchison was Henry Hobson Richardson, a follower of the Neo-Romanesque style who even established in North America his own style, the so-called 'Richardsonian Romanesque'. The corner pillars of the clock tower are topped with pinnacles and balustrades. Beneath them on all sides of the open space housing the bells are balustraded arches. The Neo-Byzantine nave and the chapel with its large demi-rose window are decorated with 20 stained-glass windows by Louis Comfort Tiffany.

Philipp Meuser

La Maison OGILVY

1307, rue Sainte-Catherine
Ouest
David Ogilvy
1894–1896

037 C

In 1866 James Angus Ogilvy founded the department store that bears his name in the heart of the city. Later he had his son David design a new building. This five-storey store follows the principles of the Chicago School and is distinguished by its steel frame. The façade of undressed stone and the enormous arched windows on the ground and fourth floors likewise made the flat-roofed building an attraction in the Montréal of its day. In 1909–1910 the department store was extended. After several changes of owner over the years, today this listed building belongs to the Holt Renfrew chain and offers mainly luxury brands. A planned extension by the architects Jeffrey Hutchison & Associates Inc. in cooperation with Lemay Architects envisages a façade lift. This will hopefully see the end of the green shimmering reflective-glass with which the windows are currently glazed. With 250,000 square metres of shop space Ogilvy will be one of the largest luxury shops in North America.

Philipp Meuser

Bibliothèque Redpath
815, rue Sherbrooke Ouest
Sir Andrew Taylor
1893

038 C

In 1893 Montréal's first library building was given to McGill University by Peter Redpath, an industrialist who had made his money in the sugar industry. The architect, Andrew Taylor, had come to Montréal from Edinburgh. The building he designed, smaller than today's complex, was initially known as Redpath Hall and is in the Richardsonian Romanesque style (so-called after the architect Henry H. Richardson). Its façade of undressed stone is richly decorated, including with gargoyles, columns, pilasters, towers, and stained-glass in high, quasi-Gothic arched windows. Innovatively, for the book stacks Taylor used a steel frame with thick glass floors, allowing light to pass through all three floors. There were several extensions to the library, including in 1900 by Andrew Taylor again and in 1921 by the successful Montréal architects George Taylor Hyde and Percy Erskine Nobbs. What we see here today is a complex consisting of several buildings, including the McLennan Library (built 1967–1969). Together with a large tower, these edifices' gables and arched windows cluster around the original building, which is now used as a concert hall. The library's reading room was moved to part of the extended building in 1921.

Montréal History and Art Collection

Philipp Meuser

Maison Dubuc
438, rue Sherbrooke Est
Alphonse Raza
1894

039 B

This jewel-like building might seem to have been imported from the Old World. It was built for Arthur Dubuc, who was himself a builder specialising in stonework. Dubuc commissioned an asymmetrical, vertically emphasised private palace with a rounded bay-window tower, a second bay window supported by a colonnade, and a tall stepped gable. The intention was to embody a synthesis of several European styles. The entrance arcade with the balcony on the raised ground floor brought an Italian flair; the gables of the deliberately differently designed sides of the building had German or Dutch prototypes. The three-storey villa housed the private Club Canadien between 1926 and 1968. The iridescent chromatic variety of its façade was the result of combining worked grey limestone; fine, pink-coloured granite columns on the ground floor; and a green copper roof, which with its small superstructures and diverse window sizes exhibits a playfulness that is rare for Montréal. The filigree stone ornamentation on the façade is also irresistible to the eye. For several years now, however, this magic has been blunted by the adjacent 14-storey brick high-rise in whose shadows the Maison Dubuc stands for most of the day.

Heike Maria Johenning

Gare-hôtel Viger
700, rue Saint-Antoine Est
Bruce Price
1896–1898

040 C

The New York architect Bruce Price immortalised himself in Montréal with, among other things, this striking station building and castle-like luxury hotel. The ensemble, named 'Jacques Viger' after the first mayor of Montréal, is 'castle-like' primarily because the roof design is dominated by towers, pointed gables, and dormer windows. Horizontality is emphasised by two crossed-roof superstructures on the left and right and in the middle by a cone roof on a drum fringed with rows of windows and pointed towers. Comprising an entire street block, the station building with its polychromatic façade of Scottish brick and grey sandstone is supported by a round-arched arcade and a mezzanine storey, giving it a fortress-like appearance. In 1935 the railway station ceased operating and the hotel was converted into offices. Currently, the building is part of a development project (Place Gare Viger) by the Jesta Group, which intends to construct various new buildings and has been able to attract tenants such as Novartis, Lightspeed, and the Hyatt Centric Hotel.

Grand Trunk Building (Édifice Gérald Godin)
360, rue McGill
Richard A. Waite
1899–1902

041 C

Charles Melville Hays, the then president of the Grand Trunk Railway, a railway company which operated between 1852 and 1923 in the USA and Canada and had its headquarters in London, commissioned his fellow-American Richard A. Waite to design the GTR's Canadian office in Montréal. Arranged in a U shape and encompassing an entire street block, this monumental administrative building is five storeys high with two seven-storey, square corner towers. Its construction was problematic because it had to be built over a branch of the St Lawrence River. Although it belongs to the first generation of high-rises in Montréal, its round-arched windows, Ionic pilasters, and Corinthian half-columns link it to Europe, in particular to the École des Beaux-Arts in Paris. Fine garland decoration and floral ornamentation soften the massiveness of the grand structure with its tower-clock over the main entrance. Only the most expensive materials – such as grey Stanstead granite and yellow-brown limestone from Indiana – were used in its construction. The lion decoration on the right corner tower symbolises the power which this railway company possessed at the time. The same message is conveyed by the interior, where use was made of various types of marble, fine woods, and English ceramics. Financial difficulties in 1919 led to the building being taken over by the Canadian government and then in 1923 by the Canadian National Railway, which operated it until 1961. It was then purchased by the government of Québec. In 1987–1988 the building was renovated. Known today as the Édifice Gérald Godin, it houses the Department for Immigration, Diversity, and Inclusion.

Heike Maria Johenning

Philipp Meuser

Ancienne Bourse de Montréal 042 C
453, rue Saint-François-Xavier
George Browne Post
1903–1904

The Montréal Stock Exchange was founded in 1832 in the premises of the Exchange Coffee House. The Ancienne Bourse was built at the beginning of the twentieth century in the midst of the old city on a narrow plot of land bought from the Sulpician Order; the sales contract specified that the new building could have no windows overlooking the seminary garden at its rear. The decision to hire the New York architect George Post was a clear statement signifying a rejection of architectural influences from London, Edinburgh, and Glasgow. Post had made his name with the design of the New York Stock Exchange. He was now asked to build a smaller version of his Wall Street building in the prospering metropolis of Montréal. His answer was a Roman temple with six Corinthian columns supporting a flat cornice decorated with garlands and bearing the exchange's name and emblem. Two minitemples likewise with cornices and flat roofs were added as risalites on either side of the façade and functioned as the building's entrance and exit. Behind the columns are simple Romanesque window apertures flanked by Corinthian pilasters; these admit sufficient light into the interior. Unlike the New York exchange, this building has no opulent gable and frieze, roof balustrade, entrance balconies, or arched windows in the second storey. It also has no raised ground floor; access is almost at democratic pavement level, via five small steps. Initially the largest stock exchange in the whole of Canada, the Montréal Stock Exchange lost its leading position to the Toronto Stock Exchange in the 1930s. In October 1965 it moved to the new Tour de la Bourse (see: 096), a square high-rise that is a highly conspicuous presence in Montréal's cityscape. After French became Québec's official language for work in 1977, business increasingly moved to English-speaking Toronto. Cooperation with the stock exchanges of Toronto and Vancouver after 1999 ultimately resulted in only trading in derivatives being continued in Montréal. In 2007 the Toronto Stock Exchange bought the Montréal Exchange and was subsequently renamed 'TMX Group'. Following a renovation, the historical exchange building has since 1975 housed the Centaur Theatre, which specialises in English-speaking productions.

Heike Maria Johenning

Appartements Bishop Court `043` `C`
1463, rue Bishop
John Smith Archibald and
Charles Jewitt Saxe
1904

Houses in the Victorian Neo-Tudor style continued to be built in large numbers in Canada into the 1930s. A good example is this symmetrical, flat-roofed apartment building with a U-shaped ground plan (note that English mansions were first built around an inner courtyard, the so-called 'cour d'honneur', in the fifteenth century). The site on which this three-storey house stands was originally part of a cricket and lacrosse field. A typical Neo-Tudor feature is the narrow bay windows with vertical masonry mullions extending over three storeys. A portal, likewise of stone, links the two front parts of the building, whose shimmering red façades stand out from the standard grey of the neighbouring stone buildings. The unhewn tufa stones were probably imported from Scotland. The window surrounds of lighter sandstone give this house a festive aura, which is reinforced by the stone wreaths placed over the smaller rows of windows.

cagkansayin/iStock

Philipp Meuser

Chapelle du Grand Séminaire
044 B

2065, rue Sherbrooke Ouest
Jean-Omer Marchand
1904

Jean-Omer Marchand, who designed this building, was the first Canadian to graduate from the École des Beaux-Arts in Paris. After he returned to Montréal, the chapel for the Sulpicians' Grand Séminaire was his first important commission. Concealed behind trees and two large circular towers, the chapel stands on land belonging to a former farmhouse. Next to the Neoclassical building of the Grand Séminaire, built by John Ostell between 1854 and 1860, this elongated, rectangular chapel in the Neo-Romanesque style seems lacking in glamour. It is only in the interior with its 80-metre-long nave with arched windows that its full grandeur is revealed. The ceiling covered with exposed cedar beams has 300 intricately hand-carved recesses which draw the observer's eye upwards. The round arches in front of the altar are supported by two granite columns. The festive character of this listed religious building is also reinforced by the light colours of the Caen sandstone lining its walls. The twelve stained-glass windows were created by Gustave Pierre Dagrant (1839–1915). The fresco 'Presentation of the Virgin in the Temple' adorning the entire upper part of the choir is by the Montréal artist Joseph Saint-Charles (1868–1956).

Philipp Meuser

Philipp Meuser

Silo No 5
Pointe-du-Moulin
John S. Metcalfe
1905

045 C

Montréal's Old Port played a key role in the city's economic boom. The 1890s were a period of extensive development: the Canadian government had several piers, warehouses, and wheat silos built here. Following the opening of the Saint Lawrence Maritime Passage in 1959 and the closure of the Lachine Canal in 1970, however, the port declined in importance.

When port operations in the city centre ceased in 1976, the authorities drew up a development plan for rehabilitation of the area. Grain silo no. 5, honoured by Montréalers as an icon, is a relict of the period before 1910, when wheat grown in the west of Canada was shipped from here to America and Europe. In the decades following 1918 Montréal was the largest port in North America exporting wheat. The Grand Trunk Railway (GTR) commissioned the construction of the gigantic silo no. 5. This 400-metre-long complex consists of three elements (two

of concrete, the other of riveted steel plates) linked by aerial galleries. The construction materials precluded the risk of explosions caused by the volatile grain dust. Floating elevators made it possible to simultaneously unload inland ships and load transatlantic ships without the latter having to come into contact with the quays. On a visit to Montréal Walter Gropius praised the silos' cathedral-like but unadorned reinforced-steel structure and compared their invention with the construction of the Egyptian pyramids. Le Corbusier too considered the silo 'one of the most remarkable buildings in modern architecture.' And the German architect Erich Mendelsohn wrote of the grain elevators he visited in Buffalo, New York, that he'd seen 'stupendous verticals of fifty to a hundred cylinders, and all this in the sharp evening light, everything else now seemed to have been shaped to my silo dreams. Everything else was only a beginning.' While two other silos in Montréal were demolished at the beginning of the 1980s, silo no. 5 is currently being converted into the world's largest vertical farm.

Édifice Canadian Express
355, rue McGill
Alexander Cowper Hutchison,
George Winks Wood
1906–1908

046 C

Neo-Baroque stylistic elements are relatively rare in Montréal buildings and, where they are found, this is usually not on the façades of high-rises. The former Canadian Express building (today's Hotel St Paul), built for the Grand Trunk Railway Company, served as a prototype for office buildings of the first three decades of the twentieth century in North America. Typical of this second generation of high-rises is imitation of the structure of a classical column. Such buildings consist of three volumes placed on top of one another. The bottom two to three storeys form the base and are emphasised by a colonnade, rustication, and garlands. Storeys four to nine correspond to the shaft of the column. The top, usually tenth, storey is elaborately decorated, like the capital of a Classical column. This façade articulation is brilliantly demonstrated by the steel-framed Canadian Express building, today listed as a monument. The middle part of the building has triangular ornamented window gables with scrolls. This theme is continued in the top storey above a sumptuous cornice emphasising the horizontal. The column shaft of the middle part is, as is traditional, relatively simple, with smaller windows. Resembling a New York skyscraper, the Canadian Express building is linked underground with neighbouring buildings which likewise once belonged to the Grand Trunk Company. In 1927 the maximum eaves height in Montréal was raised to 20 storeys. Henceforward, so-called 'skyscrapers' made the cityscape more American. The city has the Montréal-born architect Alexander Hutchison to thank for several prestigious buildings, including the Redpath Museum (see: 027).

Philipp Meuser

Appartements Linton (Le Linton)

047 B

1509, rue Sherbrooke Ouest
Samuel Arnold Finley,
David Jerome Spence
1907–1908

This Beaux-Arts ensemble consisting of three volumes on a shared plinth in a prime location in the Golden Square Mile was at the time of its construction the largest apartment block in the whole of Québec. On a square ground plan rises a ten-storey monumental complex whose façade is clad with granite, terracotta, and ornamentation of baked clay. The two bottom storeys are clad with dressed granite blocks. Above them is an emphatic string course, reinforced by a lighter string course above the seventh storey and then by an imposing principal cornice and an additional cornice on the penthouse storey; the cornices and string courses create strong horizontals. Consoles, bay windows, and wreaths draw the eye to the upper part of the façade and give the house a distinct grandeur. The entrance in the form of large arched doors decorated with keystones and a cast-iron canopy also looks dignified, even if there is no raised ground floor. This high-class complex offered already at the beginning of the twentieth century what we today understand by the term 'serviced apartments'. Service staff and a concierge were included in the rental price, as were central heating, elevators, and cleaning. Residents could dine in a large dining room on the ground floor; room service was also available, however.

Musée McCord
690, rue Sherbrooke Ouest
Percy Erskine Nobbs/
Nicolet Chartrand Knoll Ltée
1908/1992

048 C

Percy Erskine Nobbs is regarded as one of the most important Canadian architects of his time. Even if he left behind him only a few buildings, these have shaped the city that we see today. Born in Scotland, he grew up in St Petersburg, was educated at Edinburgh University, and initially worked for a time in London. In 1903 he came to McGill University as a lecturer in architecture. The university approached him during his first year of work and asked him to design a building for the students' union. The simple rectangular building he created

from characteristic grey Montréal limestone was in 1967 converted into a museum of Canadian history housing the extensive collection of David Ross McCord (1844–1930), including paintings, manuscripts and documents, textiles, and objects illustrating the lives of Aboriginal Canadians. Also exhibited here is the renowned Notman photo archive (mostly already digitalised; listed as UNESCO world documentary heritage since 2019). In 1989 an annex was commissioned and funded by the McConnell Foundation. Construction of a twin building corresponding to the original structure both in size and façade material but with much fewer window openings was completed in 1992. This air-conditioned annex houses the museum's archive.

Heike Maria Johenning

École des Hautes Études Commerciales (HEC)

535, av. Viger Est
Gauthier & Daoust
1908–1910

049 B

At the time of its construction this university building was 'the most beautiful and most stately of its kind in the whole of North America', according to the architectural historian François Rémillard. The Montréal Chamber of Commerce founded the École des Hautes Études Commerciales (School of Higher Commercial Studies), an elite Franco-Canadian business school, in 1907 and specified a French architectural style for its building. And what style could better express power and influence in stone than the style of the École des Beaux-Arts from Paris? For almost 60 years this imposing four-storey building was home to Canada's first economic university. The massive cornice and two string courses on the façade emphasise horizontality; equally dignified is the two-storey portico rising above the socle storey with its arched windows. Columns and a roofline group of sculptures representing the gods Ceres and Hermes adorn this temple of knowledge, which has a J-shaped footprint. The curved side of the building likewise has columns. Inside the building, there is an atrium fringed by galleries. After several extensions and conversions the HEC moved into a new building (Campus Decelles) in 1970. In 1996 it acquired a further building (Campus Sainte-Catherine; see: 121) on the territory of the Université de Montréal. Today the HEC's original building houses the National Archive of Québec.

Philipp Meuser

Ritz-Carlton
1228, rue Sherbrooke Ouest
Whitney Warren, Charles Wetmore/
Provencher_Roy
1911/2012

050 C

This idiosyncratic Belle Époque building with a forged-iron canopy over its entrance was the first Ritz Carlton hotel in North America. The Swiss hotelier César Ritz licensed the use of his name for a fee of $25,000, having already had great success with the Hôtel Ritz, which he operated in Paris from 1898 forwards, and the Carlton Hotel in London (from 1899). The American architects Warren and

Wetmore designed a relatively simple eleven-storey high-rise with two string courses delineating the two-storey base. Baroque bull's-eyes and wide segmental-arch windows in the lower part of the façade are the only decoration on the exterior membrane. From the start the standard features offered by this luxury hotel included ensuite bathrooms, 24-hour room service, and a kitchen on each floor. The hotel's large suites have accommodated countless members of royalty, film and pop stars, and politicians, including Winston Churchill, Charles de Gaulle, Marlene Dietrich, Liberace, Tyrone Power, and Maurice Chevalier. The

Philipp Meuser

Philipp Meuser

Stephane Groleau

relatively intimate lobby has always radiated the sophisticated cosiness of a private club. Some hotel guests even resided here, in the chic Golden Square Mile, for several months at a time. In 1916 the first transcontinental telephone conversation with Vancouver was initiated from this building. Difficult times soon followed, however: the stock-market crash of 1929 was followed by the Great Depression and ultimately by World War II. In 1947 the building was sold to the French hotelier François Dupré, who turned it into a kind of gentleman's club. Media attention only returned to the hotel when the Hollywood stars Elizabeth Taylor and Richard Burton married here in 1964. In 1992 the complex was sold to the Kempinski Group. It retained its name, however, as well as the lion emblem. In 2012 Montréal's last remaining luxury hotel finally entered the modern age: an extension added to the side of the building now nestles like a kind of glass rucksack on the historical building. This design made it possible for local architects Provencher Roy to both fully preserve the façade and create additional space for 45 luxury apartments. Further space is provided by a two-storey superstructure.

Philipp Meuser

Édifice Coronation
1391, rue Ste-Cathérine Ouest
John Harold McDowell,
Peter Henderson
1911

`051` `C`

The Chicago School enriched world architecture with a new type of building: the skyscraper, i.e. a building with more than ten storeys and a steel frame. In 1871 a large fire almost completely destroyed the centre of Chicago, which at that time still predominantly consisted of wooden buildings. The city centre had in a short time to be rebuilt incorporating as much office space as possible. The façades initially remained historicist: columns and arches disguised the buildings' modern interiors. The

second phase involved experiments with metal and other finishes. Strips of windows with windows that were wider than they were high were also an innovation of the Chicago School. It was only after 1927, however, that this type of building really came into its own in Montréal, after the permitted eaves height was raised to 20 storeys. The four-storey Édifice Coronation has an exaggerated cornice, likewise a typical feature of the Chicago School. The façade of this simple department store is faced in terracotta and has segmental-arched windows and keystones above the fourth-storey windows. The dark windows with longitudinal mullions stand out impressively against the light stone, giving the building a heightened dignity.

Musée des Beaux-Arts
1379, rue Sherbrooke Ouest
Edward and William Sutherland Maxwell
1912, extensions: 1939, 1975, 2011, 2016

Today Montréal's Museum of Fine Arts occupies an entire street block. Four extensions have been added to the original building. The ensemble's foundation stone was laid by William and Edward Maxwell with a stylish Neoclassical temple building with a four-columned entrance colonnade. The marble for the façade cladding was specially imported from Vermont. William Maxwell dedicated himself to the École des Beaux-Arts style after working for several years at the architecture firm of Jean-Louis Pascal in Paris. He also had the good fortune of being on hand to experience the Exposition Universelle (world's fair) of 1900. He made sketches of the Grand Palais and Petit Palais, the two showpieces for this style, and then returned with his impressions to Montréal. Perfect symmetry and ornamentation were especially important to him. His brother, Edward, was responsible for the interior fittings. The brothers' perfectionism was such that each of the Ionic columns of the entrance arcade had to be hewn from a single block of marble; each column weighed 26 tonnes. The valuable freight was loaded onto a train in Vermont and then transported from Gare Windsor (see: 029) to the building site on four trucks. The museum building is notable for its two window friezes and emphatic cornice. In 1939 an annex was added to a design by Harold Lea Fetherstonhaugh. In 1976 a further pavilion in the Brutalist style (Pavillon Liliane et David M. Stewart) was erected. All the buildings are connected underground. Also linked are the Erskine and American United Church (see: 036) opposite and the glass pavilion erected in 2011; together, these structures form the Pavillon Claire et Marc Bourgie and are likewise part of the museum complex. The museum now encompasses more than 50,000 square metres of exhibition space. A bridge into the future has been established by Jodoin Lamarre Pratte Architectes (together with Atelier TAG) with their annex with its façade of aluminium louvres. Since 2016 visitors to the Pavillon Michal et Renata Hornstein (named after its sponsors) have been welcomed by a gallery building consisting of two square, staggered glass cubes. 4000 square metres divide into six light-filled and entirely wood-lined storeys. A curtain of aluminium slats breaks up the glass façade and offers glimpses of wooden stairs that have been freely arranged in the space and of an 'events staircase' on the bottom three floors. The transparency of the new building, which has won various prizes, creates a connection with the exterior world and provides an ideal setting for, among others, the 75 works of art gifted by the Hornsteins.

Philipp Meuser

Édifice Unity
454, rue De La Gauchetière
Ouest
David J. Spence
1912–1913

053 C

David Spence was educated at M.I.T. in Boston and at the École des Beaux-Arts in Paris. Here, on an L-shaped ground plan, he designed a visionary factory and office building with a reinforced-steel skeleton as its core. Stylistically, this ten-storey high-rise looked to the structure of the classical column – the measure of all things for many high-rises of this time. The 'base' is formed by two storeys faced with ashlar. The 'shaft' stands out for its red brick and large leaded windows, which admit abundant light into the interior. A row of arched windows topped by a powerfully overhanging cornice forms the 'capital'. The roof is flat. Now converted into a residential building, the Édifice Unity is a fine example of the Chicago Style of architecture, a movement which produced mainly modern high-rises built using new materials.

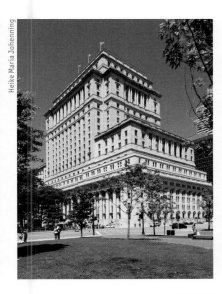

Édifice de la Sun Life   054 C

1155, rue Metcalfe
Frank Darling and John Pearson;
Charles Barry Cleveland
1913–1918; 1923–1925; 1929–1931

This gigantic flagship building – for many years the largest building ensemble in the British Empire – was erected in three stages; its central, 24-storey, flat-roofed section was completed only in 1931. Resembling an oversized wedding cake, the 122-metre-high complex is clad with 43,000 tonnes of granite. Even from a distance one can make out the imposing three-storey granite columns high up on the middle part of the building; similar columns decorate the side wings and the ground floor. Altogether, 114 Ionic and Corinthian columns were installed. Cornices and string courses give the building a strong horizontal emphasis. Apart from an austere order of pilasters facing the Cathédrale Marie Reine du Monde (see: 020), there is no other ornamentation. The architects, Frank Darling and John Pearson, also indulged their fondness for elaborate columns in the interior, which is, even without the columns, richly decorated with bronze and marble (including Noir Belge from Belgium, Pink Tavernelle from Italy, and pink marble from Tennessee). During World War II the Sun Life Building acquired unexpected and ironic importance when Winston Churchill decided to have

the British reserves of gold and money transported to Canada as a precautionary measure. Could there have been a better place to store these valuables than in this oversized safe? A secret operation named 'Fish' saw the treasure shipped from Liverpool to Halifax. Halfway across, however, the HMS *Emerald*, a light cruiser with the precious freight on board, ran into exceptionally heavy seas and was forced to slow down. When the ship eventually arrived, the money continued its journey from Halifax to Montréal, where it was stored in the basement of this building and guarded by the Royal Canada Mounted Police, while the gold reserves were kept in Ottawa. This operation was the largest transaction of its kind to date. The money was never to return to Europe but was gradually invested in the New York Stock Exchange in order to pay off Great Britain's war debts. None of the then 5000 employees of the Sun Life Company, which offered financial and insurance services, ever suspected this cuckoo's egg in the building's cellars. In 1977 Sun Life's office was moved to Toronto, after French was declared Québec's official working language and Toronto became Canada's financial centre. The vast ensemble of the Sun Life Building also includes a bell-tower, whose peals can be heard every day at 17.00. The building itself is regarded as Canada's crown jewel or, at the very least, as one of its most outstanding edifices.

Heike Maria Johenning

Maison Marchand
486, av. Wood
Jean-Omer Marchand
1913

055 B

The rural district of Westmount contains many private villas – including, in a quiet side-street, the villa of the highly decorated Montréal architect Jean-Omer Marchand. Marchand was the first Canadian to graduate from the École des Beaux-Arts in Paris. He initially specialised in religious buildings (see: 044) and worked together with many different colleagues, including in later years Ernest Cormier, whom Montréal has to thank for

a special variant of Art Deco. We can only speculate as to why Marchand designed his own house in the Neo-Tudor style, which derived from England. Possibly, he had prosperous anglophone and anglophile clients in mind, to whom he looked for new commissions. However, large façade apertures had always been important to him; his two-storey villa seems to consist mainly of expanses of glazing. The left side of the building is dominated by a glorious supersized window with side- and cross-mullions of the kind that is typical for this style. Above it is a cartouche in light-coloured sandstone. The dark entrance door under the Tudor arches with the small wrought-iron balcony above it is slightly set back, allowing the right side of the building to step forward again and show itself to its best advantage. Here arched windows on the ground floor are topped by a wooden veranda running across the second storey. In general, Marchand here uses light sandstone to emphasise the red brickwork. This elegant combination of materials is also typical of the Neo-Tudor style.

Maison Clarence de Sola
1374, av. des Pins
Saxe & Archibald
1913

056 B

Between 1900 and 1939 Montréal witnessed the construction of exotic buildings borrowing from Egyptian, Byzantine, or, as in this case, Moorish architecture. Clarence de Sola, the client for this house, came from a family of Sephardi Jews which originated from Spain and had come to prominence in Québec; his father was a distinguished rabbi, philanthropist, and professor at McGill University. A fervent Zionist, Clarence was chairman of Montréal's Jewish community and later of the Canadian Zionist Federation. In a fit of nostalgia he had the well-known Montréal architects Saxe and Archibald design a private palace with Moorish horseshoe arches and terracotta cladding. Because the house is built on a steep slope, only four of the eight storeys in its rear part are visible from the street.

The asymmetrical composition is accentuated by a square observation tower extending one storey above the roof; like the central part of the complex, this is covered with a hipped roof of orange clay roof tiles. The round-arched windows and entrance door are decorated with rich arabesques. The interior too is in the Moorish style, with arcades and loggias. The sparse, very small windows give the building a Mediterranean feel. Today the Maison Clarence de Sola is the residence of the controversial society Opus Dei.

Heike Maria Johenning

Heike Maria Johenning

Édifice Joseph-Arthur Godin
2112, boulevard Saint-Laurent
Joseph-Arthur Godin
1914

057 C

Joseph-Arthur Godin (1879–1949) left behind him only a few buildings, but they include some of the most original in Montréal. Today he is considered one of the pioneers of Modernism in North America, even if he was also a master of the École des Beaux-Arts style, to which he kept returning. One of Modernism's prime achievements was the reinforced-concrete skeleton, which Godin brought to Canada with this corner house. The rounded corners on all sides also make this building unique in the surrounding cityscape. The elongated block has been perfectly adapted to the slope on which the house stands: its front part drops a storey. Expansive rounded corner balconies, a three-storey loggia over the main entrance, and wrought-iron balconies make this one of Montréal's few examples of Art Nouveau. The building was originally intended as an apartment block; however, when Godin went bankrupt in 1915, it was used for other purposes, including as a clothing factory. Today it is a hotel. A modern five-storey extension with a façade of dark-grey artificial stone has an aluminium roof structure that extends above the historical building in a protective gesture. The original wrought-iron spiral staircase has been wrapped in Plexiglas, like a museum exhibit, so as not to jeopardise the status of this architectural monument.

Philipp Meuser

Heike Maria Johenning

Église Saint-Michel-Archange et Saint-Antoine
058 B

5580, rue Saint-Urbain
Aristide Beaugrand-Champagne
1914

Hardly anyone would suspect that this eye-catching structure with its large flat dome (diameter: 23 metres), a main portal rising above the nave, and a minaret-like clock tower is in fact a Catholic church. The religious building in the city's Mile End district was designed by the architect and artist Aristide Beaugrand-Champagne originally for Montréal's Irish-Catholic community. Taking the Hagia Sophia in Istanbul as his model, the eccentric architect devised a unique building with a cruciform ground plan. It is not just the use of dark-red brick as façade material that is untypical for Montréal. The decoration, which mainly consists of round-arched windows with lighter-coloured surrounds, is complemented by a rose window over the entrance and an enormous semi-circular stained-glass window in the aisle. The dome is decorated with a fresco by the Italian-born painter Guido Nincheri showing a scene from the life of Archangel Michael. A statue of St Patrick and the shamrock inset above the masonry entrance arch are today the only reminders of this building's Irish past. Today the Église Saint-Michel-Archange et Saint-Antoine is used by Montréal's Polish community and is the spiritual centre of this district, which was once home to workers and immigrants.

Heike Maria Johenning

Bain public de Maisonneuve
059 E

1875, av. Morgan
Marius Dufresne
1914–1916

The small town of Maisonneuve to the northeast of Montréal was founded in 1883 with the idea that it should become a model industrial city, 'Canada's Pittsburgh'. This ambitious goal involved more than making Maisonneuve a centre of industry (mainly manufacture of shoes and textiles, but also food production and shipbuilding): the city authorities decided to lay out areas of greenery and build boulevards and prestigious public buildings in an attempt to create a more pleasant environment. As the new community's town planner, the architect Marius Dufresne built, among other things, a market-hall and this public bathhouse (Le Bain Public et Gymnase de Maisonneuve) reminiscent of a Roman thermal bath. Large arched entrances, an overhanging cornice, and an imposing Corinthian portico make this temple of bathing a showpiece for the École des Beaux-Arts style to this day. Another typical feature is the roof balustrade with its sculptural decoration by the sculptor Arthur Dubord. Financial difficulties resulting from World War I led to Maisonneuve being incorporated into Montréal in 1918. Today it is part of the Île de Montréal.

Château Dufresne
4040, rue Sherbrooke Est
Marius Dufresne, Jules Renard
1915–1918

The Dufresne family, which had a flourishing construction business, built itself this imposing house in the Neoclassical style. To design it, the client, Oscar Dufresne, looked no further than his brother Marius, who worked as an architect in Montréal. Marius collaborated with the Parisian architect Jules Renard and took his inspiration from the Petit Trianon in Versailles. The result was a symmetrical mansion divided into two identical parts (occupied by the two brothers' families) with an opulent façade composed of paired Ionic columns, two risalites, and four balconies. Above a magnificent cornice a balustrade defines the roof edge. This small castle possesses vast grounds. To meet the taste of the francophone elite, Dufresne and Renard opted for stylistic elements from the Parisian École des Beaux-Arts style. The interior is in the Louis XV and Louis XVI styles, even if each room was decorated differently. Paintings by the Italian-born Canadian artist Guido Nincheri decorate the ceilings. The original marble, a pool with nymphs, and period furniture have been preserved. A staircase connects the two halves of the house. Today the Château Dufresne is a museum.

Michel Bussieres / dreamstime

Chiesa della Madonna della Difesa

6810, av. Henri-Julien
Louis Roch Montbriant
1919

061 D

Standing in the middle of Little Italy, this church, untypical for Montréal and of enormous dimensions, was commissioned by immigrants from the Italian region of Molise and is named after the apparition of the Madonna in the village of La Difesa. A Neo-Romanesque/Neo-Byzantine building rises above a ground plan in the shape of a Greek cross. It has a rounded corner, a lattice dome, and three pointed-gable superstructures that give it a great height. The main material is red brick; the decorative elements, including lesenes (pilaster strips) emphasising the church's height, are of sandstone. All three gable sides have rows of small round-arched windows. Additionally, three large rose windows admit abundant light into the interior. Listed as a monument in 2002, the Chiesa della Madonna della Difesa is famous far beyond Canada's borders for its rare frescoes. The glass- and fresco-painter Guido Nincheri worked for 30 years on the unique ceiling paintings. For the apse he created a group picture commemorating the signing of the Lateran Treaty by Benito Mussolini in 1929: it shows Il Duce on a horse, surrounded by dignitaries from the Catholic Church.

Heike Maria Johenning

Entrepôt frigorifique
1000, rue de la Commune Est
John S. Metcalfe & R. Percy
1922

062 B

In the Old Port, not far from the Pont Jacques Cartier and the Molson Brewery, looms a vast, 150-metre-long building completed in 1922 as storage for perishable goods being transported through Montréal's port. Occupying an entire street block, this nine-storey reinforced-concrete structure was at the time of its construction one of the largest cold stores in the country. State-of-the-art equipment permitted calcium chloride to be cooled in an attached powerplant which no longer exists today. The cold air was purified using ozone and then piped through the building. Some of the rooms were heated with steam so foods could be stored at room temperature in winter. The red-brick façade has ochre-coloured blind arcades. Pilasters of light sandstone form a subtly varied rhythmic pattern contrasting with the brickwork. Large segmental-arched windows decorate the two bottom storeys. The four multi-storey square roof towers used to contain lift machinery and water tanks for the sprinkler system. Today, following the building's reconstruction for residential use, these superstructures have been converted into lofts; their harbour views make them some of the most beautiful penthouse apartments in Montréal.

Édifice Ernest-Cormier   063 C

100, rue Notre-Dame Est
*Charles Jewett Saxe, Louis-Auguste
Amos; Interior: Ernest Cormier*
1922–1925

This grand Neoclassical court building has an opulence which is especially noticeable from a distance. Fourteen austere Doric columns stretching over three storeys form an impressive colonnade housing the entrance to this temple; the intention must have been to call to mind the architecture of ancient Athens, the cradle of democracy. The Latin inscription on the architrave reads: 'Frustra legis auxilium quaerit qui in legem committit' ('Those who break the law seek its help in vain'). The semi-circular niche housing the tall bronze entrance doors and the diversity of chandeliers in the interior bear the mark of the architect Ernest Cormier, who developed the Art Deco style in Montréal and whose buildings shape the city's face to this day (the Université de Montréal is just one of his works; see: 065). After Cormier's death in 1980, the building was named after him. Justice was carried out here until the 1960s; subsequently, the building became the residence of the Conservatoire de musique et d'art dramatique du Québec. In 2002–2005 the building was renovated. Since then, the Court of Appeal has met here.

Théâtre Rialto
5711, av. du Parc
Joseph-Raoul Gariépy,
Emmanuel Briffa
1923

064 B

This is one of the last surviving movie houses in North America from the era of silent film. Its architect, Joseph-Raoul Gariépy, had worked as an assistant to the influential Montréal architect Theodore Daoust, whose partner in business he later became. There are a number of important buildings in Montréal by Gariépy. This almost symmetrical, strictly articulated flat-roofed building stands out for its large segmental-arch ground-floor windows and arched windows extending two storeys above the entrance and the exit at the left and right of the façade. Above each of the latter windows rises a segmented broken pediment decorated with a cartouche. The two pediments are connected by a balustrade decorated with vases. This heavily ornamented Neo-Baroque building has similarities with the Opéra Garnier in Paris (1861–1874). Particularly captivating is its middle section, where five

French windows are framed by balconies and Corinthian half-columns standing on small consoles; between the windows rise two-storey-high Corinthian columns, between whose capitals are five large œils-de-bœuf. The influence of the École des Beaux-Arts is unmistakable. The interior, on the other hand, alludes to Art Deco, which in North America took hold later than in Europe. Here we find garlanded friezes and bas-reliefs, as well as pilasters decorated with masks. The large mosaic windows and elaborate murals are the work of Emmanuel Briffa, an artist originally from Malta who decorated a number of theatre buildings in Montréal and almost 100 in Canada as a whole. From the top tier you get a good view of the 1300-seat auditorium, which today mainly glows a dark red colour. In addition to film showings, music and theatre events were also held here. In the period after World War I cinema buildings were almost as important as the films shown in them: the public came to experience a total illusion. Part of this effect was the semi-circular canopy with chains of lights and billboards projecting above this building's entrance.

Université de Montréal
2900, boul. Édouard-Montpetit
Ernest Cormier
1924–1932/1942

065 B

The process of obtaining approval for a Catholic French university dragged on for decades. It was only in 1920 that the Université de Montréal – founded in 1878 as a branch of the Université Laval in Québec City – was able to break away from its mother institution and commission a new building. The global economic crisis, however, postponed implementation once again. The main building of this vast ensemble on a plateau on Mont Royal was finally inaugurated in 1943. The well-known Montréal architect Ernest Cormier broke with the tradition of designing public buildings in the Neo-Gothic style and created an exceptional – and, at the time, controversial – Art Deco building with a dominating central tower instead of a chapel. The materials used in its construction were modern and visionary. Beige-coloured bricks replaced the traditional grey Montréal limestone as cladding for the reinforced-concrete structure (Cormier claimed that the use of yellow brick from Ohio made it possible to 'give the walls a richer look'); red marble was used for the entrance doors. Also new was the way in which the vertical strips of metal windows were slightly recessed. The 16-storey square tower housed elevators and ventilation shafts, as well as stacks of books. The vertical windows and masonry pillars make the tapering tower with its flat dome seem even taller. Here Cormier was inspired by the Empire State Building, which was completed in 1931. Symmetrically arranged around the towered centrepiece, the university buildings occupy an area of six street blocks. The grandeur of the pioneering design is reflected in the interiors, also the work of Cormier, who paid great attention to finishes, colour, and lighting. The concrete load-bearing structure has largely been left exposed. The Hall of Fame and the amphitheatre are true Art Deco masterpieces with stepped ceiling lights, pillars of black marble, vertical neon chandeliers, and curved buttresses.

2

The Chicago School and Art Deco

Nicolas Mc Comber/iStock

Heike Maria Johenning

Philipp Meuser

Oratoire Saint-Joseph du Mont-Royal

066 B

3800, chemin Queen Mary
Dalbé Viau, Alphonse Venne, et al.
1924–1967

Standing on an eminence on Mont Royal, this cruciform Roman Catholic church is one of the most important pilgrimage sites in North America, the largest church in Canada, and a superlative religious building in all respects. Its origins, however, lie in a small chapel, only 4.5 by 5.5 metres, built by the miracle-healer Brother André. The chapel was expanded four times before André collected donations sufficient to pay for a basilica dedicated to his patron saint, St Joseph. The 60-metre-high polygonal dome with a diameter of 39 metres is the second-largest dome in the world after St Peter's in Rome. It rests on a drum pierced with a ring of windows and is flanked by four small turrets. The Neoclassical portico with a Corinthian colonnade and a semi-circular window topped by a triangular pediment made its appearance in one of the first design sketches of 1916.

The church was only completed, however, in 1967, after being worked upon by numerous architects, including for a time Lucien Parent and Gérald Notebaert. The church rises above a socle storey with arched windows and an observation platform. The focus, however, is not the granite-lined modern nave with its stained-glass windows and dome above an octagonal footprint, but the votive chapel. Here a statue of St Joseph presides over an unending sea of candles amidst a solemn silence. The coffin of Brother André is displayed in the crypt.

In 1954 the church was elevated by the Pope to the status of *Basilica minor*. The large organ, to this day considered one of the ten most outstanding organs in the world, was built by Rudolf von Beckerath Orgelbau of Hamburg. Renovation work has included the installation of escalators and elevators. Currently, a 360-degree observatory with elevator and ramp is being built in the dome (Atelier TAG, Architecture49). Scheduled to open, together with a new entrance foyer, in 2024, this is already being advertised as 'the highest window in Montréal'.

Appartements Le Château
1321, rue Sherbrooke Ouest
Ross & MacDonald
1925

This prestigious ensemble consists of three identical individual buildings with turrets and corner towers. Here the name is the programme: 'Le Château' designates a high-class residential building with 140 apartments on 14 floors. Pamphile Réal du Tremblay, the owner of the newspaper *La Presse*, commissioned this apartment building for the city's wealthiest class. In addition to spacious apartments with state-of-the-art fittings, the complex offered a concierge and valet service. Elevators and fireplaces were likewise part of the standard furnishings. For the extraordinarily simple façade, horizontally emphasised by two wide string courses and vertically by narrow corner towers, use was made of Tyndall stone specially shipped from Manitoba and Indiana limestone (for the architectural details). The light colour of the high-quality limestone makes this ensemble, which occupies an entire street block, an exception in its surroundings. The architects, Ross & MacDonald, had made their name with important buildings in Toronto. Here they inserted a veritable monument into an upscale neigbourhood which already included the Musée des Beaux-Arts (see: 052), built on the opposite side in 1912, and the Ritz Carlton (built in 1911; see: 050).

Philipp Meuser

Philipp Meuser

Heike Maria Johenning

Bain Genereux/
Écomusée du Fier Monde
2050, rue Atateken
Jean-Omer Marchand
1926–1927

068 B

Jean-Omer Marchand, the architect of this Art Deco jewel, was born in Montréal but lived in Paris from 1893 to 1903. There he developed a taste for the innovative ideas of European architects. Upon his return to the St Lawrence River, he initially encountered only clients who were interested in the Beaux Arts style. After an excursion into the Neo-Tudor style, in which he dressed his private house (see: 055), a tender for a public bathhouse in the 1920s at last gave him the opportunity to experiment with Art Deco. The city of Montréal had decided to build a public bathhouse in each working-class neighbourhood in response to a 1905 report that 75% of housing in such districts had no bath or shower. Marchand took his cue from buildings by the French architects Louis Bonnier and François Hennebique, whose works included the design for the Butte-aux-Cailles swimming pool in Paris (1924). The façade of ochre-coloured tiles and polished sandstone was, however, Marchand's own invention. Typical of the Art Deco style is the simple exterior membrane, decorated only with a few curves in the masonry, a geometrical tile pattern, and elaborately placed keystones. The mascaron above the basket arch of the entrance door of this two-storey building was intended to keep evil spirits away. The windows and doors, additional decorative elements on the roof, and metal sign are, typically for Art Deco, in black. The oval flat roof supported by buttresses is of aluminium covered in copper. The reinforced-concrete skeleton made it possible to create a large interior space with enormous round arches for the swimming pools and seating for 400 visitors. In 1980 the listed and fully renovated bathhouse was converted into a district museum. On the floor of what used to be the pool, a permanent exhibition looks at the triumphs and tragedies of an industrial and workers' district.

Philipp Meuser

Théâtre Empress

5560, rue Sherbrooke Ouest
Joseph Alcide Chaussé,
Interior: Emmanuel Briffa
1927

069 A

The discovery of the tomb of the Ancient Egyptian Pharaoh Tutankhamun by the British archaeologist Howard Carter in 1922 drew enormous attention worldwide and led to a true Egyptomania in art, film, fashion, and design. One of the rare architectural testimonies to this enthusiasm for Egypt in Canada is the Empress Theatre. This four-storey temple of cinema has a square ground plan. The eye-stopper on its façade of brick and stone chippings is a monumental portico stretching over the second and third storeys. Of intricate design, this has Egyptian-inspired columns and pilasters with palm-frond capitals, reliefs of hieroglyphs by the sculptor Edward Galea, and two mascarons in the form of heads of Ramesses. The designer Emmanuel Briffa (see: 064), known for his elaborate interior decoration for cinemas, designed the interior furnishings. In 1992 a fire destroyed the premises. Since then, the building has been closed and its structure has deteriorated. In 2020 the authorities declared the building unsound. In 2021 various parties put forward proposals for renovating and reactivating this architectural monument.

Philipp Meuser

Heike Maria Johenning

Édifice Bell
1050, Beaver Hall Hill
Barrott & Blackader
1927–1929

070 C

With the completion of this 96-metre-high office building Montréal's business centre moved one step further in the direction of Dorchester Square, away from the Notre-Dame quarter in Vieux-Montréal. The Bell Telephone Company of Canada was based in Toronto. For its Québec headquarters in Montréal Barrott and Blackader opted for a Neoclassical design with a square ground plan. Taking the place of the Église Saint-Andrew, a Gothic church with a fine bell-tower which stood on this site from 1851 to 1927, this 22-storey high-rise with recesses at the corners and large arched windows on the ground floor tapers towards the top, giving it a vertical emphasis. The risalites stretching to the ninth floor on all four sides end with elongated balconies. Pilasters accentuate the middle part of the façade and the upper three storeys. Overall, this flat-roofed building, clad in natural stone, has elegant proportions and a sublime grace. The interior is elaborately decorated with marble and bronze. Today the Édifice Bell is surrounded by high glass towers and so is not immediately noticeable. The building's architects, Barrott & Blackader, also designed the Édifice Aldred (see: 075), an experiment with the Art Deco style. A certain resemblance between the two buildings is nevertheless impossible to miss.

Tour de la Banque Royale
360, rue Saint-Jacques
York and Sawyer,
S. G. Davenport
1926–1928

071 C

At the beginning of the twentieth century the rue Saint-Jacques was Montréal's Wall Street. After spending six years buying up the entire street block between rue Saint-Jacques and rue Notre-Dame, the Royal Bank of Canada built itself a spectacular headquarters here: a 22-storey, steel-framed, Neoclassical skyscraper clad with grey limestone and with a socle storey of granite. This 121-metre-high building was in 1928 the tallest in the British Empire and the first allowed to rise higher than Notre-Dame Cathedral (see: 006). In 1962 the bank moved to the skyscraper Place Ville-Marie. Later, the banking hall on rue Saint-Jacques became a co-working space with a café. Today it is mainly hipsters you meet here.

Heike Maria Johenning

Édifice des Tramways
155, rue Saint-Antoine Ouest
Ross and Macdonald
1928

072 C

The famous tandem of architects Ross and Macdonald designed this massive high-rise for the company Tramways de Montréal. The ten-storey clinker-brick building has a regular grid of windows, floral friezes, and a ground storey marked off by a string course and pierced by display windows. The structure's verticality is emphasised by a roof balustrade with small sandstone pointed gables shaped like petals which seem to shoot into the sky on pilasters placed between the windows. Borrowings from the Arts and Crafts movement are to be seen in the pilaster friezes in the lower storeys and in the foyer decoration of plasterwork and metal trim. In the upper area of the façade the architects switched to mechanically produced repetitive patterns. The four building corners end one storey lower, drawing the eye to the pinnacle-like roof tops.

Masonic Memorial Temple
1850, rue Sherbrooke Ouest
John Smith Archibald
1928–1929

073 B

For decades it was difficult for the Freemasons to gain a foothold in strongly Catholic Montréal. With this temple building in the city centre, in almost direct proximity to the Grand Séminaire (see too: 044), the association finally acquired a visible presence in the cityscape. This Neoclassical building with its enormous portico and Ionic columns nevertheless maintains a certain restraint: there are no symbols of Freemasonry on the façade. The scarcity of window openings gives the main façade a mysterious appearance. The architect, John Smith, had immigrated from Scotland and won his spurs at the well-known architecture firm of Edward and William Sutherland Maxwell before setting up his own practice with his colleague Charles Saxe. Together with Saxe, he created a number of idiosyncratic buildings in Montréal, including Bishop Court Apartments (see: 043).

Édifice Dominion Square/
The Gazette
1010, rue Sainte-Cathérine
Ouest
Ross and MacDonald
1928–1930

BalkansCat/iStock

As a counterpole to the Sun Life building (see: 054), which is likewise situated in Square Dorchester, this distinctive high-rise built on a rectangular ground plan and clad with Rockwood limestone from Alabama seems a little small. This, however, is an optical illusion: 12 storeys high in its middle part, the Dominion Square Building occupies an entire street block. Seen from a bird's eye perspective, it consists of three blocks linked by a further transverse block and a shared plinth. This creates two small and two large inner courtyards which, however, only begin above the plinth storey and admit abundant light into the offices on the upper floors. Due to the division of the main block into three parts, there are hardly any rooms without windows. Situated in a prime location and fitted with state-of-the-art technology, the complex contains one of Canada's first shopping arcades, situated on the bottom two floors. When it opened in 1930, this was the first building with escalators in Montréal. The idea of combining a shopping arcade and offices was absolutely revolutionary, coming decades before modern skyscrapers found their way to Montréal. Vast round-arched portals and display windows aimed to attract shoppers, while the three avant-corps mainly housed office spaces. The Québec tourism office and editorial office of *The Gazette*, the only English-speaking newspaper in Montréal, were also based here. Four underground storeys provided ample space for parking vehicles, while eight automated elevators ensured fast access to the office floors. The façade design with its truncated building corners, round-arched windows on the top floor, and elaborate ornamentation with cornices and string courses has an Italian feel.

Heike Maria Johenning

Édifice Aldred

501–507, place d'Armes
*Ernest Isbell Barott
(Barott & Blackader)*
1929–1931

075 C

Montréal's first Art Deco skyscraper dominates the city's skyline to this day. This elegant, 96-metre-high building in the direct vicinity of Notre-Dame Cathedral (see: 006) was completed two years after the restriction prescribing a maximum of ten storeys for building height was lifted. As in New York, however, flat-roofed setbacks typical of the Art Deco style were prescribed by law to ensure that tall buildings let sufficient sunlight into the streets below. The central block of the pyramid-like Aldred Building is 23 storeys high and steps backwards in four setbacks. The steel frame is supported by a three-metre-thick concrete mat two storeys below ground level. The uniform façade design is vertically emphasised by strips of windows (840 in all) and soaring buttresses that resemble limestone pilasters. The lower façade area is decorated with metal friezes and bas-reliefs depicting pines and maples. The skyscraper owes its name to the man who commissioned it: John Edward Aldred, the then president of the Shawinigan Water and Power Company. The interior too was state of the art for its time in terms of building equipment. The central vacuum-cleaning system, electrical timer clock, system for burning rubbish, paper baler, and ozone machine to eliminate odours in the kitchen were all at this time novelties in Montréal. The decoration of the interiors and the foyer with diverse types of marble (including Belgian Black, Yellow Sienna, Tinos Greek, St Genevieve Golden Vein, Verde Antique, and Moutonelle), bronze, terrazzo, and cast iron emanated respectability, as did the six elevators lined with teak.

Philipp Meuser

Édifice McDougall et Cowans   076 C
500–520, rue Saint-Francois
Xavier
James Cecil McDougall
1929–1930

This Art Deco building was commissioned by the Anglo-American Trust Co. The architect, James Cecil McDougall, designed an unusually narrow seven-storey building whose most important and most modern distinguishing feature is the vertical strips of windows with metal frames. The cladding is limestone from Queenstown (Ontario). At the tops of the two flanking towers are bas-reliefs representing Prosperity (a young woman holding a horn of plenty), Labour (a young man at work), and Finance (a young man holding a globe). These are by Henri Hébert, the son of the Canadian sculptor Louis-Philippe Hébert. Henri Hébert also created the bas-reliefs over the strips of windows; these depict symbols of prosperity, such as a sailboat and a railway. Until 1953 the lower floors were home to the brokerage firm McDougall & Cowans, which owned the Anglo-American Trust Co. Founded in 1900, McDougall & Cowans was one of the largest brokerage firms in Canada, with offices in Halifax and Vancouver. The upper floors mainly housed law firms. Today there are residential lofts here.

Maison Ernest Cormier   077 B
1418, av. des Pins Ouest
Ernest Cormier
1930–1931

This architectural icon nestles modestly, almost invisibly, up against an incomparably more sumptuous neighbouring building. Two cubes of different heights placed next to one another hardly lead one to suspect that this jewel built on a slope has three further storeys at the rear. The flat-roofed structure with its smooth concrete façades articulated only by a long strip of windows without string courses or cornices is radically modern. An Art Deco frieze draws the gaze above the central window. The Art Deco interior, for the most part designed by Ernest Cormier himself, is still in its original condition. It includes wallpaper, mahogany furniture, and tiles with floral décor. At the beginning of the 1980s Pierre Elliott Trudeau, former prime minister of Canada, had this house carefully restored. He lived here from 1983 until his death in 2000.

Heike Maria Johenning

Philipp Meuser

Édifice Archambault
510, rue Ste-Catherine Est
Raoul Gariépy
1930

078 B

This filigree high-rise made of light-coloured sandstone was commissioned by Edmond Archambault, the founder of the music seller Archambault Musique. Until 2018 this six-storey corner building with its curved corners, geometrical window friezes, and the cornice-less flat roof that is typical of Art Deco was the so-called 'House of the Future' – the headquarters of the Archambault chain of shops selling music and subsequently books too. Features that were very modern at the time of this building's construction were the two-storey, metal-framed display windows on the ground floor and the polygonal metal canopy over the entrance. The classic neon sign with white letters on a black background was returned to the façade only recently in recognition of its importance to Montréalers. This listed building, part of a chain of 15 branches, has belonged to the media mogul and politician Pierre Karl Péladeau (owner of the media business Québecor) since 1995. Péladeau was determined to preserve the neon sign as part of the city's visual heritage. At night it now once again glows in classic Hollywood red.

Heike Maria Johenning

Caserne de pompiers et poste de police #10

1684, boul. de Maisonneuve Ouest
Shorey & Ritchie
1931

079 B

In the 1930s so many fire stations were built in the Art Deco style in Montréal that many people saw them as synonymous with this style. In this instance we see a flat-roofed corner building erected as part of a campaign to relieve unemployment following the difficulties of the late 1920s. Clad with limestone, it is marked by a square tower rising three storeys above the rest of the complex. Such towers were typical of the time; their vertical apertures made them a good place for drying fire hoses after fire-fighting operations. Fire Station No. 10 is a three-storey cube flanked by two two-storey cubes. A strip of flowers in place of the traditional cornice, four two-storey-high decorative windows with metal frames, and a finely executed bas-relief over the entrance lend this otherwise simple building a touch of elegance. In 1931 Fire Station No. 10 was awarded the Prize of the Royal Architectural Institute of Canada.

Philipp Meuser

**Caserne de pompiers
et poste de police #23**
521–523, place Saint Henri
Ludger Lemieux
1931

080 B

This impressive fire station in the Art Deco style is the little sister of the Marché Atwater (see: 085), likewise designed by Ludger Lemieux. Three storeys high and clad in red clinker brick with decorative elements in artificial stone, Caserne 23 captivates the eye with its curving roof line, clinker buttresses emphasising the vertical, and expressive, helmeted drying tower. The latter, capped by a polygonal copper dome, has a vertical, recessed strip of windows and long fins of brick. An element of drama is created by the numerous bas-reliefs over the building's entrances; these show firemen and policemen, as well as thieves behind bars, but also represent the elements of fire and water and the god Mercury. Over the entrance on the west side is a bas-relief with the city of Montréal's motto: *Concordia salus* ('Well-being through harmony').

Philipp Meuser

Philipp Meuser

Marché Saint-Jacques

1125, rue Ontario Est
Zotique Trudel,
Joseph Albert Karch
1931

081 B

A stylistic element typical of Art Deco is the stepped superstructure of this building's volume, which bears a distinct similarity to a ziggurat, the stepped temple tower of Mesopotamia. The latter structures taper upwards towards the middle and end in flat roofs. Such pyramidal forms are frequently to be seen in Montréal; they include, for instance, the Édifice Aldred (see: 075). We find the same here: the front façade and the tower structure of this dark-brown clinker building are emphasised by a large arched window in a sandstone portal and by bas-reliefs on the truncated building corners. That this is a market hall is clear from the rectangular ground plan and the ornaments with flowers, vegetables, or fruits covering the entire façade. Also typical of buildings in this style is the flagpole on the central block.

Philipp Meuser

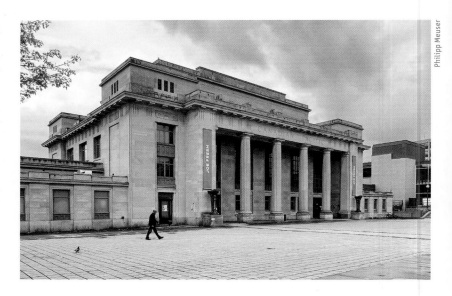

Philipp Meuser

Canadian Pacific Railway
(Métro-Station Gare Parc)
7245, rue Hutchison
Colin Minors Drewitt
1931

082 D

The headquarters of the Canadian Pacific Railway, Canada's first transcontinental railway company, is a monumental four-storey Neo-Renaissance palace which borrows from Art Deco. Erected on a rectangular footprint, it has impressive stone reliefs, metal-framed windows, and an interior which features travertine walls and skirting boards of Belgian marble.

A four-columned portico forms the entrance. On top of a mighty cornice rises a storey topped with a flat roof and pierced by a small number of window slits. In 1984 the city of Montréal purchased this majestic ensemble, which is situated outside the city centre, and revitalised part of it as a metro station. Today, if you get out at the Gare Parc stop, you can still make out the historical railway halls. Above the entrance on the west side of the building a mascaron reminds us of the original inhabitants of this country; this is the only building decoration of this kind in all of Montréal.

Philipp Meuser

Eaton's Restaurant (Le 9e)
677, rue Ste. Catherine West
Jacques Carlu; Ross and
Macdonald, Associate architects
1931

083 C

In the 1930s New York had Macy's; Montréal had Eaton's and Simpson's, both on rue Sainte Catherine, the city's main shopping street. Eaton's opened in 1927, occupying an entire city block. To attract as many customers as possible, in 1931 a restaurant was installed on the ninth storey. At the time, there was nothing like it anywhere else in the world. The interior set out to dazzle with the sophisticated opulence of a luxury liner; such was the wish of Lady Eaton, the wife of the department store's owner, an avid cruise traveller. The restaurant's decoration was the work of the architect Jacques Carlu, who dedicated himself to Art Deco after graduating from the École des Beaux-Arts in Paris. He later served as artistic advisor to the Secretary General of the United Nations for the interior design and decoration of the UN headquarters in New York. Even the foyer of this restaurant is exquisitely decorated with French marble, oak parquet, and huge portholes. The centrepiece of the strictly symmetrical 'luxury liner' is the ten-metre-high dining room, also used as a ballroom. This is decorated with 16 marble pillars, four metal balustrades, and two enormous murals (*Pleasures of the Chase* and *Pleasures of Peace*) by Natacha Carlu. Further rooms include a tea salon, a room with a fireplace, and private dining rooms. Opal glass and light slits in the sidewalls provide artificial and natural light. Also typical of the Art Deco style was the colour scheme of that time: the walls were lined with a diagonally striped, beige-pink-coloured wallpaper (replaced with a salmon-coloured paint during a modernisation). The wall paintings glow a contrasting lime-green. The original multi-coloured linoleum floor (the restaurant's 'most avant-garde aspect', according to Jean Carlu, the architect's brother) and the black marble applications have survived, as have the alabaster lights in the form of vases, the bas-reliefs created by Denis Gélin with culinary motifs, and the high tables with marble feet. A perfect symbiosis of French and American Art Deco, the restaurant stopped operating in 1999, when the department store went bankrupt. Ivanhoé Cambridge, which today owns the building, has converted its lower floors into a high-end shopping centre and office space with a central atrium. The ninth-floor restaurant, meanwhile, remains substantially untouched, its fate undecided, in a kind of enchanted sleep (thanks to its status as a listed monument). Its furniture has been put into storage.

Northern Deco – Art Deco Architecture in Montréal

EATON

Église du Saint-Esprit

2851, rue Masson
Joseph-Égilde-Césaire Daoust
1931–1933

084 E

The Church of the Holy Ghost is one of only a few Art Deco churches in the whole world. In the 1930s the French Benedictine monk and architect Dom Bellot, advising the Catholic Church on their building projects, argued for a renewal of church architecture. This explains why the innovations in this building (originally known as the Église Sainte-Philomène de Rosemont) are more than just skin-deep. The reinforced-concrete skeleton was a radical technology that made it possible to create a wide nave unobstructed by columns.

In addition to its spaciousness, the interior is notable for its stained-glass windows by Guido Nincheri. Nevertheless, the still young architect Joseph-Égilde-Césaire Daoust seems to have had a hard time mastering the new design language: the exterior with round-arched portals, arched windows, and square bell-tower above the main entrance looks at first sight very traditional. It's only at closer inspection that you see that the grey limestone façade is delicately detailed (with geometrical friezes, simple sculptures of angels, and crosses with stylised floral decor) and gradually tapers towards the top. The original Neo-Gothic spire had to be taken down in 1949 after explosions in the nearby quarries made it unstable.

Marché Atwater
110–154, av. Atwater
Ludger and Paul L. Lemieux
1933

085 B

The Montréal businessman and local politician Edwin Atwater (1808–1874) had not merely a street and a metro station named after him, but also one of the largest market halls in Canada. In response to the world economic crisis, the Montréal authorities decided to create new jobs by building public amenities and institutions. The result, at the beginning of the 1930s, was the construction of a number of very high-quality Art Deco buildings. One of them is Atwater Market in the district of Saint Henri. The square tower is visible from afar, soaring above a four-storey-high, rectangular, ochre-coloured brick building with large windows and projecting ribs. The two long sides end in a semi-circular attic. Its simple form and black-and-white colour scheme make the clock-tower an Art Deco jewel. Ludger and Paul Lemieux, the architects of this building, were father and son. Atwater Market Hall has been experiencing a revival since the beginning of the 1990s, driven partly by this area's gentrification and partly by the market's popularity with cyclists riding the path from the Old Port of Montréal to the Lachine Marina. A bicycle bridge over the Lachine Canal has vastly improved the market's accessibility.

BalkansCat/iStock

Nicolas McComber/iStock

Jardin Botanique
(main building)
4101, rue Sherbrooke Est
Lucien Kéroack
1932–1937

086 E

The symmetry and monumentality of this impressive block point to the influence of the École des Beaux-Arts. Closer inspection, however, reveals that this three-storey, red-clinker building, which today accommodates the Université de Montréal's Biodiversity Centre, is actually a genuine work of Art Deco. Two flat-roofed towers at the two corners emphasise verticality. The façade is dominated by a vast, central portal of grey limestone stretching over the entire height of the building. Two small circular domes on the roof accentuate this imaginary portico. Square friezes on the façade take up floral motifs and/or demonstrate geometrical shapes, a typical characteristic of Art Deco. The Botanical Garden was established in 1931 at the initiative of the botanist and member of a religious order Marie-Victorin Kirouac. Together with Henry Teuscher, a landscape gardener who had emigrated to Canada from Berlin, he devoted his whole life to developing this facility, which today, with its Japanese Garden, Chinese park, Insectarium (rebuilt by the German architecture firm Kuehn Malvezzi; see: 129), arboretum, and the First Nations Garden (a garden for endemic plants and plants cultivated and used by peoples indigenous to Canada), is one of the major botanical gardens in the world. Teuscher remained head curator until 1962. In 1937 a long fountain rising in several cascades was created, emphasising the central axis of the main building. A high fountain was added in 2015.

Gibeau Orange Julep
(restaurant)
7700, boul. Décarie
Hermas Gibeau/Olius P. Bois
1932/1945/1966

087 D

This walk-in orange is 55 years old and still one of the most popular buildings in Montréal. The idea for the unusual structure belonged to Hermas Gibeau, manufacturer of an orange-coloured fruit lemonade (based on a family recipe). After having had great success selling his drink at the Belton Park amusements park, Gibeau opened a fast-food restaurant – not in the shape of an orange – on rue Sherbrooke in 1932. This was followed by a two-storey sphere, coloured orange and cast in concrete, completed at the present address in 1945. A small square window on its second floor gave it a resemblance to a house in a fairy tale. When the boulevard was widened in 1966 to create an expressway, the architect Olius P. Bois rebuilt this jewel a little further from the street, with a load-bearing structure of wood and clad with fibre-glass panels. The orange's diameter was increased to 13 metres, which approximately corresponds to three storeys. Gibeau Orange Julep, incidentally, is still sold in the shops today.

JHVEPhoto/iStock

Philipp Meuser

Pharmacie Montréal
916, rue Sainte-Catherine Est
Raoul Gariépy
1934

088 B

It is only at second glance that you recognise the sublime beauty of this five-storey building. At the time of its opening the pharmacy of Charles Duquette was the largest and most luxurious of its kind worldwide. It was open 24 hours a day (until 1973); its automatic doors were installed at the end of the 1930s. Today nothing of the magnificent Art Deco display windows survives, but the original bas-relief friezes are still to be seen in the upper area of the vertically accentuated façade. In 1985 the pharmacy was sold to the drugs chain Jean Coutu; the building itself was not. Recently, this architectural monument was renovated.

Casa d'Italia
5310, rue Jean Talon Est
Patsy Colangelo
1936

 089 E

Little Italy's community centre is a modern flat-roofed building of red clinker brick with a semi-circular volume at its front. Instead of a string cornice, the two-storey building is girdled by a lightly plastered strip. Under the flagpole, a

Heike Maria Johenning

Heike Maria Johenning

stylistic device frequently used in Art Deco and intended to evoke the flowing lines of a steamship, rises a pilaster to whose lower end a bundle of lictors containing an axe is attached. These fasces were the symbol of the highest authority in the Roman Empire and were in the New Age frequently used by immigrants as a symbol of identity with ancient Rome; they were also an attribute of Mussolini's National Fascist Party. Four further bundles of rods decorate the front side of the building. Patsy Colangelo, the building's young architect, went so far as to place a vast piece of intarsia work in the form of this bundle in the foyer. For this he paid a high price: at the beginning of World War II he was arrested and spent almost a month in the city's Bordeaux Prison.

Philipp Meuser

Holt Renfrew
1300, rue Sherbrooke Ouest
Ross and MacDonald
1937

 090 C

Holt Renfrew, a luxury department store founded in Québec in 1837 originally as a fur business, decided to mark its 100th anniversary with the construction of a branch in Montréal. This building's uncompromisingly modern design immediately brought the well-known firm of architects Ross and Macdonald an award from the Royal Architectural Institute of Canada. The American newspaper *Women's Wear Daily* described the new department store as 'one of the most modern and most attractive retail establishments on this continent.' Seven storeys (originally six storeys) high, with limestone façades, a rounded and truncated corner, and an emphatic strip of

windows on the fourth floor, this is a fine example of the Art Deco style. The exterior envelope is horizontally structured, has no string courses or cornice, but is capped by the long sweep of its glazed penthouse. Above the entrance area is a two-storey-high, metal-framed window, which admits abundant light into the shop spaces. The bronze and copper fittings of the magnificent main portal exhibit depictions of various furred creatures. In the 1950s Holt Renfrew was even official furrier to the Queen of England. In 1947 an eight-storey wing was built onto the original building to a design by James Kennedy, likewise in the Art Deco style. Exclusive designer fashion is sold here, in the heart of the posh Gold Square Mile district, to this day. Holt Renfrew recently merged with Ogilvy, another Canadian luxury department store with a distinguished history.

Gare Centrale
895, Rue de la Gauchetière Ouest
John Campbell Merrett
1938–1943

The construction of the main railway station brought the first plans for development of Montréal's 'Underground City' (Montréal souterrain or Ville intérieure; officially: RÉSO) – a network of mostly subterranean links between buildings and transport infrastructure that enables Montréalers to move about their city without being exposed to the bitter winter weather. Work on the new main railway station had already begun in 1926 but was then temporarily interrupted due to the global economic crisis that began in 1929. This International Style block appears from the outside rather lacking in decoration. Inside, blue-white Art Deco bas-reliefs designed by Charles Comfort welcome travellers with patriotic scenes from Canadian history. A continuous frieze contains the English and French texts of the Canadian national hymn. The elongated station building is flanked on both sides at the front by staircase towers which rise two storeys above it. Horizontal strips of windows locate the building in the modern age. Underneath the railway station is a shopping centre; the top storeys serve as a parking garage. Today Canada's entire fire service is run from this station.

Philipp Meuser

Northern Deco:
Art Deco architecture in Montréal

Sandra Cohen-Rose
Author of *Northern Deco – Art Deco Architecture in Montreal*;
founding president of the Art Deco Montreal society

In the 1920s and 1930s Art Deco, which drew its inspiration from a wide array of sources, was the popular architectural style in Montréal, as in many North American cities. It remains a permanent reminder of the spirit and splendour of an era which continues to haunt, fascinate, and occasionally disturb us to this day. Art Deco architecture represents an important part of Montréal's historical heritage – as was acknowledged at the 10th Art Deco World Congress in 2009. The International Coalition of Art Deco Societies granted Art Deco Montreal, an organisation founded in 2002, the honour of welcoming delegates from all parts of the world in order to commemorate and celebrate the heritage of this style. Art Deco Montreal sets itself the task of promoting the perception, evaluation, and protection of Art Deco works of art and architecture. City excursions and presentations – such as a visit to the Art Deco Moyse Hall at McGill University, where there is a notable bas-relief by the Art Deco artist Henri Hébert – are intended to demonstrate the diversity and richness of this style in Montréal.

The interaction between architecture and figurative art, an important part of the French artistic tradition, is easily recognisable in Montréal's Art Deco architecture. Look, for example, at the main building of Montréal's Botanical Garden (founded in 1931; see: 086), an example of the art of Henri Hébert. A Cubist bas-relief with culinary motifs by the French sculptor Denis Gélin and murals by Natacha Carlu, the wife of the French architect Jacques Carlu, adorn the famous restaurant installed – also in 1931 – on the ninth floor of Eaton's department store (see: 083). Due to the close historical connections between Montréal and Paris, the Art Deco style came to Montréal earlier than to most other North American cities. At the beginning of the 1920s architects in Montréal developed their own style with a unique design language: Northern Deco.

Philipp Meuser

Édifice médical Drummond, rue Drummond 1414, Architect: Percy Erskine Nobbs (1929).

Canadians' reserved character and the country's long, cold winters were responsible for Northern Deco evolving, alongside the traditional Art Deco vocabulary of urns, rising suns, and waterfalls, a uniquely Canadian symbolism involving motifs such as maple leaves, pine needles, and beavers. These often had a new simple, geometric form and were made using the latest technology. Reinforced concrete, steel, and glass offered new challenges and opportunities.

Late 1920s and 1930s Art Deco buildings often used symbolic motifs to carry more concrete nationalistic, political, educational, or commercial messages. Motifs such as fasces – a bundle of wooden rods with an axe in the middle (the logo adopted by the Fascists, Italian nationalists who came to power in Italy in the 1920s and had many sympathisers in Montréal) – joined maple leaves and flowers to reflect the political climate of the time in Québec. Radio antennas and miniature tires propelled

by wings symbolised technological advances and speed, while Greek and Roman mythological figures such as Hermes / Mercury (the god of commerce and travel) and Poseidon / Neptune (chief of the water deities) represented traditional values and morals. Symbols drawn from botany and neurology highlighted the contributions made by men and women of science.

Montréal's skyline, unlike New York's, does not abound with Art Deco skyscrapers. At 98 metres high, the Aldred Building (Édifice Aldred; see: 075), designed by Barott and Blackader in a form that resembles a falling fountain or a wedding cake, remains Montréal's iconic skyscraper. It was only erected after the city amended a bylaw that had blocked the construction of buildings taller than 39.6 metres. The amended law stipulated that buildings could exceed this height provided that they had set-backs ensuring better natural lighting and ventilation in their interiors and more sunlight

One of the largest market halls in Canada: Le Marché Atwater (opened in 1933).

Heike Maria Johenning

on sidewalks for pedestrians. During long, cold winters with limited hours of daylight, the dark shadows cast by tall buildings pose an added threat to the health of Montréalers. To let more daylight fall on the pavement, the buildings had to taper towards the top like pyramids. The disinfecting properties of ultraviolet sun rays were also eternalised in Northern Deco – for instance, through the kind of stylised sun rays you get in the Quintal Bath.

Relatively little known are the unique Catholic churches in the Art Deco style inspired by the French Benedictine monk and architect Dom Bellot (1876–1944), who was first invited to Québec in 1934. Together with many noted Montréal architects of the era, including Ernest Cormier (who designed Montréal's most ambitious Art Deco building, the University of Montréal, 1924–1942), Dom Bellot worked on Saint Joseph's Oratory, which has the second largest dome in the world.

On the one hand, Montréal churches experienced an upswing to provide a spiritual focal point for a growing Catholic population with an average of 10–20 children per family. On the other, the city had a pulsating nightlife. Cabarets and jazz cafés attracted a fast-moving crowd, many of whom were Americans looking for momentary relief from prohibition. In the 1920s and 1930s Montréal, known as 'sin city', was the largest wet city on the eastern seaboard. The Lion d'Or, an Art Deco cabaret from the 1930s, reminds us of this era to this day.

Camillien Houde (1889–1953), mayor of Montréal on and off from the late 1920s to the early 1950s, was a driver of the Art Deco era, even if his decisions to oppose conscription in 1939 and to introduce make-work projects to accelerate recovery from the Great Depression made him a controversial figure. These projects were a precursor to President

Franklin D. Roosevelt's New Deal. Among the legacy of Art Deco structures left by Houde are some of Montréal's most familiar buildings: the Montréal Botanical Gardens (see: 086), the Marché Saint-Jacques (see: 081), and the Atwater Market (see: 085), as well as a number of police and fire stations (see: 079, 080), hospitals, and public baths. During hard times, these vertically thrusting buildings, often artistically decorated with inspiring messages in bas-relief, provided not merely work for the unemployed but also hope and renewed faith in the political system.

Northern Deco occurred at an exceptionally complex time – the period between the two world wars and during the Great Depression, a troubled time which ultimately led to the collapse of many important institutions and to the rise of fascism and Nazism. Symbols of nationalism therefore abound in Montréal Art Deco architecture. In the 1950s and 1960s those who had lived through the Depression and World War II wanted no visible reminders of these miseries in the cityscape; many buildings were for this reason thoughtlessly demolished.

Not until the 1970s, after an appropriate temporal distance, were people able to properly appreciate the ornamentation and elegance of this eclectic architectural style. The term 'Art Deco architecture' was first coined in the 1960s in North America, in distinction to the term 'Art Deco' as a stylistic designation of the French and international movement in the fields of design, crafts, and figurative art, which was coined at the International Exposition in Paris in 1925. Today Northern Deco is considered a serious and valuable part of Montréal's architectural heritage: something to be understood, cherished, and unconditionally preserved.

High-rises and Tetris monsters

LES GRUES MONACO INC.

www.gruesmonaco.com
450 679-0612

Modernism and Brutalism, 1950–1980

Modernism

The opening of the Saint Lawrence Seaway in 1959 made it possible for seagoing ships to reach the inland of North America from the Atlantic. Montréal prospered and continued to grow horizontally. Between 1960 and 1976 more than a third of buildings in the city centre fell victim to street widening, construction of expressways, or erection of car parks. The completion of a skyscraper with a circular ground plan on Place Ville Marie to a design by I. M. Pei in 1962 (see: 092) marked the beginning of a new architectural era in Montréal: Modernism. Functional, no-frills buildings with concrete cladding, prefabricated components, parts made from steel and aluminium, and strip windows made it possible to serially manufacture residential buildings. The foregoing of any kind of ornamentation, cornices, and high-quality materials signified a break with the past. Suddenly, buildings sprang up in the form of cubes, spheres, or pyramids. In Montréal's Verdun district Mies van der Rohe, a German architect living in the USA, designed a petrol station (see: 100) which has similarities to the New National Gallery (Neue Nationalgalerie) in Berlin. And on Westmount Square in downtown Montréal stands one of Mies' famous high-rise ensembles (see: 099).

Montréal on the world stage

The second half of the 1960s saw the start of Montréal's second 'golden age'. The construction of the metro and of the largest underground city in the world (Ville Intérieure) released new energies. The city's winning of the right to hold the 1967 world expo led to the creation of Île Notre-Dame (an artificial island formed using 15 million tonnes of excavated rock), among various other major projects, but also caught the attention of the whole world.

Expo 67 is to this date the most-visited world exhibition of all time. It was an opportunity for renowned architects to immortalise themselves with innovative masterpieces, including Richard Buckminster Fuller with his Biosphère (see: 111) and Moshe Safdie with his Habitat 67 residential complex (see: 102). The latter brought Brutalism to Montréal. Regarded as a European-inspired reproduction of the style of the Japanese Metabolists, Habitat 67 became a catalyst for urban development. Place Bonaventure, a forbidding fortress which was in its day the second-largest commercial building in the world (see: 097), is regarded as a showpiece of Brutalism. In recent years, however, openings have thoughtlessly been made in the slabs of this formerly windowless 'concrete monster'.

Olympic challenges

The Olympic Games of 1976 bequeathed Montréal a costly but not very functional stadium and a mountain of debt. 'Without the Olympic Games the city would today be paved with golden cobble-stones,' stated The Globe and Mail in 1992. When in 1977 French was established as Québec's official language, many industries and service enterprises moved to English-speaking Toronto. The result was several referendums on the independence of francophone Québec, all of which, however, proved fruitless. When the Canadian prime minister Pierre Trudeau signed the Canadian Charter of Rights and Freedoms, Canada became formally independent of the United Kingdom. In architecture Postmodernism gained a foothold in the cityscape. The revival of historical styles brought the return of ornamentation. Buildings with granite cladding, columns, and reflective glass now entered the scene.

Place Bonaventure: a case for #SOSBRUTALISM.

Place Ville Marie
1, place Ville-Marie
*Henry N. Cobb (I. M. Pei & Assoc.);
Dimitri Dimakopoulos (ARCOP)*
1958–1962

092 C

When the New York architecture firm I. M. Pei & Associates was commissioned to design Montréal's first skyscraper, lead designer Henry N. Cobb and his team came up with an audacious idea. Montréal had been dominated by the clergy for centuries; now a cruciform ground plan was chosen as the basis for a 188-metre-high office and business complex. The design of what was at the time, at 47 storeys high, the tallest building in Montréal was regarded as a radical intervention in the cityscape and was the subject of much controversy. This was hardly surprising: the project involved building over train tracks and the construction of 280,000 square metres of space beneath street level to accommodate a shopping centre and a large food court. This underground development finally laid

Nicolas McComber/iStock

the foundation stone for Montréal's Ville Intérieure, today the largest subterranean city in the world. It also means that the 'aluminium giant', as 1 place Ville-Marie is known, can be reached without visitors having to expose themselves to wind or weather. The steel-and-aluminium tower with its curtain façade of an almost white colour and regular black strips of windows remains one of the tallest buildings in the city. The four shorter office buildings in the plaza area were part of the design project from the start but were erected slightly later, in 1963–1964. The name chosen for the skyscraper by the then mayor of Montréal, Jean Drapeau, alludes to Fort Ville-Marie, the first French settlement on the site where the city stands today. Recent incarnations of the spaces at the top of the building have included a restaurant and nightclub and a public observatory. The present owner, Ivanhoé Cambridge, is currently carrying out a revitalisation, including the erection of a glass roof over the Food Court.

Heike Maria Johenning

Heike Maria Johenning

Le Château Champlain
1, place du Canada
Roger D'Astous and
Jean-Paul Pothier, Norman Slater
1963–1967

093 C

This 610-room hotel building erected above a square ground plan is one of the few skyscrapers to be designed in accordance with the principles of Frank Lloyd Wright. In the 1950s the Montréal-born architect Roger D'Astous was one of Lloyd Wright's pupils. He was in 1952 the only Québec architect accepted for an internship at Wright's architecture firm Taliesin in Wisconsin. The convex, semi-circular window openings differ refreshingly from the monotonous strips of windows of many other skyscrapers, giving the façade a rich plasticity. These windows are why the Château Champlain is

also fondly known to Montréalers as 'the cheese-grater'. Essentially, this high-rise comprises a steel skeleton fleshed out with glass and concrete panels (a distinguishing mark of Brutalism). The ribbed concrete blocks on the other sides of the building also locate it in the transitional period between Modernism and Postmodernism. The hotel housed in the building has for many years been operated by the Marriott chain of hotels. The rooftop restaurant, closed for renovation, has recently reopened under the name 'Terrasse Belvu'. The building's architect, Roger D'Astous (1926–1998), deservedly has a firm place in the city's annals. The Canadian Centre for Architecture (CCA) looks after D'Astous' archive, which includes approximately 4000 drawings, 66 publications, and 2500 photographs of his 182 projects.

3

Salle Wilfrid-Pelletier

094 C

175, rue Ste-Catherine Ouest
Hazen Sise, Dimitri Dimakopoulos,
Fred Lebensold (ARCOP)
1963

Part of the Quartier des Spectacles cultural complex, this ensemble was built at the peak of Brutalism in the 1960s. The multifunctional hall, which, with almost 3000 seats, is the largest in Canada, is named after the Canadian pianist and conductor Wilfrid Pelletier, who was for many years the artistic leader of the Orchestre symphonique de Montréal.

Of architectural interest is the combination of two completely different volumes. The central part is a block with rounded corners housing the auditorium. Nestled around it in a horseshoe configuration is a glazed front structure with a peristyle of vertical white struts; this contains the foyers. The inside block, which is clad with prefabricated panels of white concrete, rises several storeys above the volume in front of it. This elegant concert hall, part of the architectural heritage of Montréal's Modernism, is regarded as an icon of Brutalism and is a listed monument.

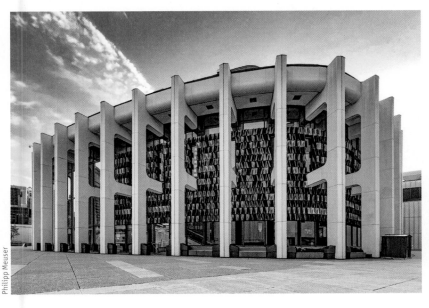

Complexe Desjardins
150, rue Ste-Catherine Ouest
Jean-Claude La Haye et associés;
Darling, Pearson and Cleveland;
Blouin et associés; Gauthier, Guité et Roy
1963–1976

`095` `C`

An ensemble of four high-rises with a hotel and office spaces, apartments, and small shops occupying a total floor area of four million square metres, the Desjardins complex is the largest piece of real estate in Montréal and even has its own postcode prefix (H5B). The originality of this isolated-looking, asymmetrical complex, named after Caisses Desjardins, an association of savings banks, is primarily a matter of its spatial configuration: it is built around a central plaza and a north-south main axis. This concept was developed by Jean-Claude La Haye, the 'father of Québec urban planning'. First, a multi-storey podium was built over a square ground plan; this contains a large and varied shopping centre. Rising on top of the plinth are four towers which increase in height in a clockwise direction. The 27-, 32-, and 40-storey high-rises contain offices; the smallest, 20-storey, 'tower' is a polygonal hotel

building which has housed the DoubleTree by Hilton since 2019. It stands out visually from the higher towers thanks to the chequerboard-like arrangement of its rows of windows. This Brutalist ensemble is clad with the ribbed concrete panels that are typical of this style; the panels have a coarse-grained surface structure. The subtle octagonal shape of the three taller towers increases the number of corner offices and imparts a saving lightness to the monumental complex. The storeys in the plinth structure form a public plaza covered with a transparent dome. In view of the city's cold winters, this area with cafés, cinemas, and shops has from the start been very popular with Montréalers. High walls of glass based on a French model resist the winds without the need for metal frames. Escalators and corridors provide access to Montréal's sprawling underground city (this is the easternmost

point of access to the Ville Intérieure), allowing Montréalers to travel to and from Desjardins without having to step out into the cold. All in all, this slightly forbidding complex is an integral part of the Montréal cityscape.

Heike Maria Johenning

Tour de la Bourse
800, place Victoria
Pier Luigi Nervi, Luigi Moretti
1963–1964

096 C

At 150 metres high, the 47-storey building erected for the Montréal Stock Exchange is to this day one of the tallest in the city. Three window-less in-between floors serving as technical storeys divide it visually into four sections. The bottom section comprises only four storeys and may therefore also be treated as the building's socle. The edges of light-coloured concrete define the volumes, allowing them to be perceived visually as a single unit. At the same time they serve as pillars and stand out from the bronze-coloured, anodised-aluminium expanses of the façades. The Tour de la Bourse was designed in the International Style by the Italian architect Luigi Moretti and his fellow countryman, the structural engineer Pier-Luigi Nervi, and has become an integral part of the city's skyline. Moretti and Nervi seem to have taken great care with the building but to have paid less attention to the surroundings and the local climate. Its almost black shimmering façade means that the building's interior has to be cooled with elaborate air-conditioning equipment. And, despite its undeniable originality, the tower does not suit its immediate surroundings, which consist of rather low buildings and small areas of vegetation. Originally, three high-rises of this type were to have been erected on this site, but the plan was discarded for financial reasons. An extensive renovation was carried out in 1995.

Place Bonaventure
800, rue de la Gauchetière Ouest
Raymond T. Affleck (ARCOP)
1964–1967

097 C

This once-in-a-century building is a powerful fortress with a square ground plan. Occupying 288,000 square metres of space (an entire street block), it was at the time of its construction the second-largest commercial building in the world, with a programme that included offices, retail businesses, exhibition halls, garden areas, parking spaces, and a hotel with an outside pool. The requirement that the 18 railway tracks that run through the site should be built over proved an especially difficult challenge. Additionally, a connection had to be created with the metro and thereby also with the main railway station on the adjacent site (see: 091). Raymond T. Affleck, who later joined forces with colleagues to form a working group under the name ARCOP, graduated from the McGill School of Architecture in Montréal and specialised in the kind of visionary Brutalism that came from Europe. He also designed the Stephen Leacock Building on the McGill Campus. His statement 'What Italy can do with marble and stone we can do with wood and concrete' reveals his unqualified faith in new materials. Nevertheless, the realisation of this 16-storey building proved difficult in many respects. The railway tracks, for instance, remained in operation during the construction work; holes were drilled down in the spaces between them to the layer of rock underneath so as to anchor the concrete foundations. The load-bearing structure fanned out into vast beams with ceiling/floor panels. An innovative system of detachable concrete formwork allowed both a degree of plasticity and a shorter construction time. The design incorporated almost no windows: with the exception of the top four storeys, the building was clad with vertically grooved and bush-hammered concrete panels. This in turn gave it a hermetic and forbidding character. The exterior gives no indication of its greened interior courtyard, which contains a second office building and the Hotel Bonaventure. Place Bonaventure played an important role as a catalyst for Montréal's urban development. Rather unintentionally, this colossus laid a foundation stone for the development of Montréal's underground city (Ville intérieure), today a system of tunnels extending over 32 kilometres and the world's largest underground city. In 1998 Place Bonaventure was renovated at a cost of 60 million Canadian dollars; window apertures were inserted on all four sides of the building. In 2018 other concrete panels were removed from the façade in order to accommodate even more windows. This violation of the complex's original character has brought supporters of #SOSBrutalism to the barricades.

Roberto Conte

Pavillon Thérèse-Casgrain
2450, boul. Eduard-Montpetit
Papineau Gérin-Lajoie Le Blanc
1964–1965

098 B

At the beginning of the 1960s a surge in numbers of students led to a need for new accommodation on the Université de Montréal campus. Several dormitories were erected. The building named after Thérèse Casgrain, a Canadian politician and advocate for women's rights, was for many years allocated exclusively to female students, which explains its nickname 'the Tower of the Virgins'. This elegant 16-storey high-rise has a triangular ground plan. Its sculptural façade has won it a reputation as a masterpiece of Brutalism. Vertical strips of windows stretch from bottom to top of the building but are scarcely recognisable as windows because their regular apertures are concealed by angular dividers. Verticality in this concrete monolith is additionally emphasised by pointed corners that project above the roof. An innovative system of separable concrete formwork creates additional plasticity in this 'pavilion' built on a plinth of stone. The concrete is unadorned, without facing or colouring.

3

Westmount Square
Westmount Square 1
Ludwig Mies van der Rohe with
Greenspoon, Freedlander and
Plachta & Kryton
1964–1967

099 B

From 1930 forwards the German architect Ludwig Mies van der Rohe led the Bauhaus in Dessau and, after the latter's closure in 1932–1933, the Bauhaus as a private institute in Berlin, before emigrating to the United States in 1938. In Chicago Mies developed his own, unique style which was mainly based on combining glass and black metal with a modern load-bearing structure of steel. When the building regulations required that the steel skeleton be surrounded with a layer of five-centimetre-thick fire-proof concrete, Mies encased it in metal and gave his buildings a façade which exposed the load-bearing structure underneath. The metal structure also proved beneficial in stiffening the exterior membrane and in minimising the effects of heat and wind. At Westmount Square he designed a residential and office complex with three staggered towers

(22, 21, and 21 storeys high), as well as a low glass cube with a flat roof. The ensemble with curtain façades of anodised aluminium and smoked-glass windows stood originally on a travertine plinth, which was replaced with granite blocks at the end of the 1980s. One of the three towers is used as an office building; the two others are residential buildings. The prototype for this design was Lake Shore Drive Apartments in Chicago (1951), where Mies for the first time employed a curtain façade and a load-bearing structure made entirely of steel. He retained this concept in the future for all high-rises of similar construction. However, he very soon moved the outer load-bearing posts back from the façade to inside the building and suspended the façade in front of them. In the Verdun district of Montréal Mies built his first and only petrol station (see: 100), which has similarities with the Neue Nationalgalerie (New National Gallery) in Berlin. It consists of two glass volumes that are independent of one another. On the Île des Sœurs, one of Montréal's islands, there are three other residential high-rises designed by Mies van der Rohe.

**Station-service
de Mies van der Rohe**
201, rue Berlioz (Verdun)
*Ludwig Mies van der Rohe/
FABG Architects*
1966

100 **A**

The opening of the Pont Champlain in 1962 was the starting signal for development of the Île des Sœurs (Nun Island), which lies southwest of Montréal. The city of Montréal bought this sandy island, today part of the district of Verdun, from the Catholic Church in 1956 for 3500 CAD and went on to commission an ambitious master plan for the area in the 1960s. The commission was given to the Chicago firm Metropolitan Structures, which had already realised several projects with Mies van der Rohe. Almost unknown is the fact that, in addition to Westmount Square, a residential and office complex in downtown Montréal (see: 099), the great Modernist architect built three further residential buildings (201, rue Corot, and 100 and 200 rue de Gaspé, 1967–1970) on the Île des Sœurs. Even less well known and therefore all the more unique is the gas station he designed on the same island. This has many similarities with the Neue Nationalgalerie (New National Gallery) in Berlin. In 2008 the ensemble consisting of two airy pavilions flanking a glass volume was listed as a monument and subsequently restored by the Canadian architecture firm FABG. It proved possible to recreate the cantilevered roof to the original design. The curtain façade was dismantled, and the old pumps are no more. The steel load-bearing structure with 12 massively welded steel beams and pillars was repainted black and now forms a clear contrast with the white-enamelled panels and fluorescent tubes on the underside of the roof. An automatised sun screen ensures that the louvres are either entirely open or entirely shut. Today 'possibly the most famous gas station in the world' has been reincarnated as La Station, a communal cultural centre serving multiple generations, and is an art Mecca that draws architecture-lovers from all over the world.

Théâtre Maisonneuve
175, rue Ste-Catherine Ouest
David, Barott & Boulva
1966–1967

101 C

Completed in time for Expo 67, this concrete monolith rises on an almost square ground plan like an Egyptian temple sitting atop a cascade of steps. The recessed plinth storey above a peripheral plateau succeeds in endowing this gigantic classic theatre building with a degree of lightness, which is reinforced on the building's rear side by a three-storey open front of windows framed with vertical brown metal struts. All the other sides of the building are clad with prefab concrete panels and are entirely without openings. Typical of Brutalism is the so-called 'wide corduroy' surface, which was intended to give the concrete façade greater plasticity. This theatre building contains five concert halls with a total of approximately 1500 seats. The design was regarded in its day as emphatically modern. However, the concrete has suffered badly over the years. The theatre is named after Paul Chomedey de Maisonneuve, who founded Montréal in 1642.

Habitat 67

2600, av. Pierre Dupuy
*Moshe Safdie with
David, Barott, Boulva*
1966–1967

102 B

'How shall we live in the future?', the overarching theme for the Montréal world's fair of 1967, occupied one young architect so much that he devised a hypermodern, 12-storey housing estate to answer this question. Habitat 67 was intended to combine the advantages of living in an apartment with every inhabitant's wish for their own garden and easy accessibility. Moshe Safdie's ground-breaking idea – to design a kind of Lego city (as he himself said, 'We bought everything that Lego made over the course of a year') from exposed-concrete cubes stacked one on top of another and prefabricated using the most modern technology – continues to serve architects from all over the world as a prototype to this day. The 354 concrete boxes were cast externally in 15 sizes and then completed on site with the addition of kitchens, bathrooms, window frames, and doors before being lifted into place using a crane; they each weigh between 70 and 90 tonnes. These residential modules have two or three rooms and are fitted with air-conditioning and central heating. Each of the 158 residential units has a garden situated on top of a neighbouring

Roberto Conte

box. The resulting agglomeration is a kind of terraced building made from staggered boxes, between which are airy free spaces which admit sufficient light into the apartments. The service areas and parking places have connections with a street. There are also play areas on the upper levels to keep children from going out of their minds. Connecting paths and bridges are laid out in such a way that people can always get to their apartments without getting their feet wet. Habitat 67 was considered the prototype of a housing concept for industrial nations. The apartments were in 1986 gradually sold to their inhabitants. Ultimately, although the concept was regarded as visionary, it was rarely copied, partly due to reasons of expense. Even if this 'concrete building set' is described as Brutalist, Moshe Safdie has explained that, 'stylistically,' he was not 'interested in concrete, nor in the aesthetic of Brutalism'; it was much more about him creating something individual so as to distinguish himself from his colleagues. The apartments are now unaffordable luxury residences for minimalists with an appreciation for the quiet location and excellent views. The architect himself purchased one of the penthouse apartments, had it renovated in the original style, and today offers visitors the opportunity to take a look behind the scenes of this icon of Brutalism.

Roberto Conte

Roberto Conte

Hôtel Le Germain
2050, rue Mansfield
Lemaymichaud (redesign)
1967/2021

103 C

This narrow, 15-storey building was Montréal's first boutique hotel after having been initially used as the headquarters of the Ordre des ingénieurs du Québec (an association of Canadian engineers). A 30-million-dollar renovation project announced by the Germain Group in 2018 and carried out by Montréal architects Lemaymichaud involved updating the original concrete façade and comprehensive renovation of the interiors. A six-storey concrete box faced in glass and steel was built onto the top of the building to house an additional six floors. A cantilevering glass lobby was added to the second floor. The original façade design owed its expressive plasticity mainly to its alternation of rows of window apertures set individually in concrete frames with rows of rimless strips of windows. Additionally, the window apertures were set far back in the otherwise undecorated, brutalistically sober high-rise. In 2021 the façade was given a make-over by the Canadian wall-painter/muralist Michelle Hoogveld, who painted it in 80 colours arranged in a colour gradient in a pattern which she called 'Dazzle My Heart'.

Philipp Meuser

Bibliothèque McLennan
3459, rue McTavish
Dobush, Stewart & Bourke
1967–1969

The seven-storey McLennan Library is one of the 'bastions' of McGill University. Wide, recessed windows give this Brutalist building a resemblance to a game of Tetris. The façade consists of identical prefabricated concrete elements fastened to a reinforced-concrete frame. An elevated walkway links the building to the distinguished Redpath Library (see: 038). At the present time, the main entrance is situated at the southern end of the concrete terrace. All traffic between floors is taken care of by the central staircase and by elevators. The library houses the Humanities and Social Sciences Library, the largest branch of McGill University Library. The sixth floor is home to the university's archive. The McLennan Library is named after Isabella McLennan, who made a large donation to the university to purchase books.

Roberto Conte

Édifice Decelles
5255, av. Decelles
Roland Dumais
1970

This massive concrete giant, nick-named 'the Bunker', made its appearance when Brutalism was already on the wane. Although mainly popular in the 1960s, Brutalism remained on the architectural scene until the beginning of the 1980s. The style is characterised by bulky, nested concrete boxes which are intended to convey power, modernity, and respect. The Decelles Building of HEC Montréal, Canada's oldest economics university, needed additionally to have the appearance of a bulwark against the political unrest occurring in Canada at that time. The five-storey, flat-roofed building originally had no window openings on its bottom three floors. In 1958 a sixth storey was added. During a renovation project carried out in 2011 rectangular glass verandas were inserted into three sides of the building on the ground floor so as to admit more light into the interior. The glass cube over the main entrance was also added at a later date. Until that point, a peripheral band with light slits in the third storey and a few narrow strips of windows beneath them were the building's only light sources. The surfaces of the prefabricated, deeply furrowed concrete panels give the Decelles Building the corrugated look that is one of Brutalism's characteristic features.

Stade Olympique

4141, av. Pierre de Coubertin
Roger Taillibert
1971–1976/1987

106 E

The history of the construction of Montréal's stadium for the 1976 Olympic Games has many similarities with BER, the new airport that opened outside Berlin in October 2020. It is not for nothing that the Olympic Stadium is known as 'the big O' or 'the big Owe' – on the one hand, an allusion to its oval shape; on the other, to the debt that was its main legacy (the initial estimate of 250 million CAD transmuted into an eventual price tag of 1.4 billion). The original design involved the construction of a sliding roof covered with a Kevlar membrane. This, however, proved unstable and too low and so was subsequently replaced with a taller, closed roof. Additionally, inflation, the oil-price crisis, and construction defects constantly postponed the building's completion. At the opening of the games neither the stadium nor the adjacent mast, the world's tallest inclined tower, were ready, so the Olympic events almost had to be moved to Mexico. The specially hired Parisian architect Roger Taillibert, who had designed the Stadion Parc des Princes (1972) in Paris, had to make a change of scale for this stadium; as a result, some of the concrete ribs simply fell off. Furthermore, a 55-tonne concrete beam toppled over. Only the bottom part of the tower serving as a mast holding the roof cables could be cast from concrete. For the construction of its upper half use was made of steel plates; this was not the original plan. Ultimately, the 175-metre-high tower was developed into an observation tower (completed in 1987) and was fitted with an ascending and descending

cable railway with double-decker gondolas on its exterior wall. At 166 metres there is a platform from which viewers can see the Olympic Village (see: 109). It was only 30 years after the Olympic Games that the debt incurred by the stadium's construction was finally paid off. In 1998 a translucent blue Aramid roof was installed instead of its precursor; this may, however, need to be replaced again. The Olympic Stadium is today used mainly for concerts and trade fairs.

Philipp Meuser

Pavillon Liliane et David M. Stewart/Musée des Beaux-Arts

3410, av. du Musée
Fred David Lebensold (ARCOP)
1973–1976

The Pavillon Liliane et David Stewart was erected on a rectangular ground plan as an extension of the Musée des Beaux-Arts (see: 052). Consisting of several concrete cubes interlocking at right angles with peripheral strips of windows at the rear, this pavilion is a typical example of Brutalism. Elevator shafts soar dramatically above the four-storey flat-roofed building. A cantilevering cube with vast panes of glass contrasts with the window-less areas of the other cubes. Since the building's construction, ivy has spread over the façade of exposed concrete, which has weathered and turned dark-grey over the years. A peripheral terrace 'hanging' above the entrance protrudes from the front wall.

Philipp Meuser

Heike Maria Johenning

Biodôme

4777, av. Pierre-de Coubertin
*Roger Taillibert, André Daoust/
Kanva and NEUF architectes*
1973–1976/1989–1992/2017–2020

What is today the Biodôme was originally erected as a velodrome for the Olympic Games of 1976. At that time Brutalism, considered modern and uncompromising, was the definitive architectural style. The French architect Roger Taillibert, who also designed the adjacent Olympic Stadium (see: 106), took his cue from the stylistic preferences of the time. His velodrome is a distinctive circular building whose convex surfaces, seen from a bird's-eye perspective, evoke the outline of a ray fish. The flattened structure seems to be supported by a circular substructure. The elongated area between the substructure and the envelope is entirely glazed. Vast octagonal window apertures provide the interior of this massive concrete building with daylight. A major conversion between 1989 and 1992 saw the velodrome reopen as a museum of ecology: the Biodôme (Espace pour la vie: Space for Life). The Biodôme offers a chance to explore four ecological systems of the American continent. A major renovation in 2020 exposed the building's concrete pillars and created new levels which can be reached by elevator. The roof construction is now visible from the ground floor. The individual ecological systems are separated by four-metre-high white fabric panels. A four-metre-high clay cliff was built for macaws to nest in. A 15-metre-long ice tunnel leads to an area that recreates conditions on the Sub-Antarctic Islands and the Labrador Coast. The tunnel takes its energy supply from geothermal sources.

3

Roberto Conte

Village Olympique
5111–5333, rue Sherbrooke Est
Roger D'Astous,
Luc Durand
1974–1976

109 E

The Olympic Village was built for the summer games of 1976 to provide accommodation for almost 9000 athletes. This dormitory town is in the Brutalist style with concrete as the main material. It consists of two blocks of buildings, each of which is grouped around a 70-metre-high tower. The two slightly staggered blocks are 600 metres long but taper upwards in terraces which become increasingly short. The deeply recessed windows of the 980 apartments give the ensemble a mystical but also hermetic grace. Following the end of the games, apartments in the complex were made available for rent from 1979. After the listed complex ended up in private hands in 1998, it was extensively renovated in 2013. Today the four half-pyramids are a popular residential address.

Philipp Meuser

Le Rigaud
425, rue Sherbrooke Est
architect unknown
1973–1976

Originally designed as a hotel complex, this massive concrete monolith is today managed by the Société d'habitation et de développement de Montréal (SHDM). In a curious way this 20-storey-high structure resembles the layered horizontality of a Chinese temple. A distinctive feature is the curving roof struts cast from exposed concrete. Above them, additional storeys resting on columns seem to float like penthouses over the rest of the building with its identical terraces. The bottom three storeys form a kind of podium with narrow windows set in masonry. In the 2000s the façade was refreshed with a vertical red band of colour which differs pleasingly from the coarse-grained, unornamented concrete panels and even imparts to this massive building a degree of lightness. Today Le Rigaud is a home for the elderly but also houses professional artists and writers participating in an exchange programme.

3

Roberto Conte

Expo 67: the most-visited world exhibition of all time

Man and his World

World exhibitions have been held since 1851 and continue to take place to this day. In the nineteenth and twentieth centuries, however, they had an entirely different significance because, having no Internet, the world offered people very few opportunities to survey the inventions and discoveries that were taking place in countries other than their own. The major world exhibitions in London (1851) and Paris (1889), for instance, displayed the attainments of the Industrial Revolution. Following World War II, in 1958 Brussels was the venue for the first expo of the new era. To this day the Atomium is a reminder of this world exhibition's thematic focus: the atomic age. The following world expo, planned for 1967 and thus in the middle of the Cold War, was initially awarded to Moscow. However, financial pressures and ideological concerns that an event of this kind could bring western ideas and customs into the country caused the USSR to withdraw its candidacy in 1962. The choice of the then comparatively little known but thriving Canadian port city of Montréal to host the exhibition marked the beginning of a new era in the city's history. Montréalers and potential visitors to Montréal were promised nothing less than the creation of an artificial island (Île Notre-Dame), the erection of a new bridge (Pont de la Concorde), and the construction of a new metro line – and all this in the same year in which the nation was simultaneously to celebrate the centenary of Canada's founding and the 325th anniversary of Montréal.

With a firm eye on the future, the world exhibition in Canada presented, above all, discoveries from the fields of science and technology, especially innovations from space travel. 'An expo like a Star Trek film,' summed up the Canadian newspaper *The Globe and Mail* in 2007. With 50 million visitors, it was to be the most-visited world exhibition of all time. In the space of just five years the cosmopolitan small port city was to be transformed into a modern metropolis.

Two islands, a bridge, and a metro line

To connect Montréal's inner city with the exhibition sites and to transport visitors inside the territory, extensive

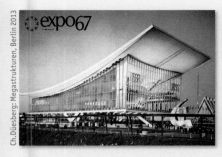

The USSR Pavilion (architect: Mikhail V. Posokhin) attracted the most visitors and was later re-assembled in Moscow. Habitat 67, a spectacular residential complex built as a modular system, on the contrary, stands in its original location to this day.

3

transport infrastructure was built, including the Expo Express, a monorail line, and a metro system. Jean Drapeau, the then mayor of Montréal, used the excavated soil to build an artificial island, Île Notre-Dame, in the Saint Lawrence River and to enlarge the existing Île Sainte-Hélène. This project was not uncontroversial, especially since there was no real compelling shortage of undeveloped land in Canada. In the space of only ten months 15 million tonnes of earth were moved and transported by vehicle over the Pont Jacques-Cartier to the site. The Pont de la Concorde was additionally built to provide a link to Île Sainte-Hélène specially for the expo.

Île Notre-Dame remains to this day a recreational resort with a beach and artificial lake. But it is also an Eldorado for Formula 1 fans: this is where the Canadian Grand Prix is held every year. Both islands are connected by bridges with one another and with Île de Montréal. All in all, the exhibition territory amounted to a spectacular 365 hectares.

Between 1962 and 1967 an entire metro system was built with three underground lines. 82% of the equipment was made in Canada. However, help with designing trains with pneumatic tyres came from the builders of the Paris metro.

The decision to build a new island from reclaimed land had the additional advantage that visitors to the exhibition did not get to see Montréal's shabbier streets. The city centre was only affected to the extent that a cultural centre was built on the Place des arts. Opposite the entrance to the port, on a pier which had been built towards the end of the nineteenth century as a shield against storms and ice floes and was later renamed 'Cité du Havre', sprang up what was at the time the most spectacular and most visionary residential complex in the world: Habitat 67 (see: 102).

As at every world expo, the 90 national and thematic pavilions served not only as visiting cards for each participating country but also for purposes of propaganda and promotion of tourism. From 28 April to 27 October 1967, 62 countries addressed the theme 'Terre des Hommes: Man and his World'; their response was to exhibit mainly new capabilities for mastering future challenges in the fields of architecture, space, and transport. The inspiration was the book of the same name by Antoine de Saint-Exupéry,

Heike Maria Johenning

Alexander Calder named his sculpture *L'homme* after the motto of Expo 67.

published in France and the USA in 1939. A quotation from this book – 'To be a man is to be responsible: to be ashamed of miseries you did not cause ... to be aware, when setting one stone, that you are building a world' – was very popular in the 1960s.

The logo for Expo 67 consists of eight identical abstract pairs of people, who form a circle and so symbolise universal friendship among the nations of the world. This original symbol was the work of the Canadian industrial designer Julien Hébert. Alexander Calder, a US-American sculptor, created a sculpture from nickel with the title *L'homme* ('The Man') to welcome visitors to Île Sainte-Hélène. Twenty-one metres high, it was one of the architectural landmarks at Expo 67.

Architecture: three-dimensional framework structures and tent roofs

The temporary character of Expo 67 was emphasised in many pavilions by the use of structures that were quick to assemble and dismantle. The most popular were three-dimensional frameworks: structures assembled from rods and connection nodes in such a way as to need only a small number of support points

and exhibit a high degree of stability. For the most part, the roofs and walls were developed from small self-supporting units which could be assembled to create all kinds of components. The use of new building materials made it possible for larger distances to be spanned with a roof than ever before. The Canadian firm Alcan, today one of the largest aluminium holdings in the world, generously subsidised buildings at Expo 67 that were erected using aluminium frames and panels. However, the ease with which new shapes could be formed in most cases had the result that a pavilion's exterior appearance had very little to do with its interior design and with the presentation of the exhibition inside.

National pavilions and cheating

The architecture at Expo 67 got a favourable reception from the critics of the time. However, the Montréal expo also saw the kind of tricks and diversionary tactics that are usual at world expos from architects who made every effort to offer spectacular spatial impressions while concealing load-bearing structures that were often merely conventional. The French Pavilion, for instance, looked from the outside like a diverging spiral with aluminium fins. Inside, its largest exhibition spaces were situated around an open staircase that was spanned with cables and reached upwards towards a skylight. Ultimately, however, in terms of construction the pavilion was merely an ordinary concrete-frame building with eight exhibition levels. The ground floor contained a presentation by the city of Paris showing ambitious solutions in the fields of architecture and infrastructure from the *Paris 2000* project. The French Pavilion also exhibited nuclear power stations and reproductions of deep-sea worlds.

The French Pavilion has been preserved and, together with the former Québec Pavilion, which is shaped like the square stump of a pyramid, today contains the Casino of Montréal. It is thus one of the few still existing relics of Expo 67.

The attempt by the Japanese to reproduce traditional forms of construction on a larger scale in concrete while employing interior lighting to make them appear weightless met with little acclaim. Cuba and Venezuela demonstrated simple exhibition boxes, while the British Pavilion, on the contrary, set out to attract attention with pompous cladding in asbestos panels and the expo's tallest tower, crowned by a three-dimensional Union Jack.

Curtain up for Canada

The pavilion of the host nation was recognisable even from afar: an upside-down pyramid called 'Katimavik' (the Inuit term for 'assembly place') and flanked by other pavilions representing individual Canadian regions. Designed by architects from Toronto and Ottawa the pyramid had an observation terrace and a shimmering crystalline exterior skin which was intended to symbolise the minerals and metals mined in Canada. The interior contained an exhibition of local art, including paintings by Emily Carr, Paul-Émile Borduas, and Jean-Paul Riopelle and sculptures by the sculptor Sorel Etrog.

Opposite, visitors were welcomed by an enormous red-brown maple tree with 500 photographs showing Canadians at work and at leisure. The two thematic pavilions, 'Man the Discoverer' and 'Man the Producer', were designed by the Montréal architecture firm ARCOP. Québec had its own pavilion, which the New York Times called 'the Barcelona Pavilion of 1967'. Arthur Erickson, an architect from Vancouver, stacked hexagonal glulam box beams to create a 42-metre-high wooden pyramid resembling a stupa; this was the 'Man in the Community' Pavilion.

Habitat 67

Habitat 67 (see: 102) is a residential complex built on a pier belonging to the exhibition territory. Conceived as a thematic pavilion, it aimed to bring the home country greater fame. Ultimately, however, it proved a ground-breaking architectural masterpiece. Its architect, Moshe Safdie, only 29 years at the time, had been born in Israel and lived in Montréal. His residential project was a housing estate built, like a kind of Lego town, from individual cubes stacked on top of one another. Each of the 158 prefabricated units ultimately built (the original plan was for 1000 housing units) weighed between 70 and 90 tonnes and was lifted into place in the complex by crane. Today the visionary box apartments are much sought after and almost unaffordable for ordinary mortals. No architecture book on the theme of visionary architecture and/or Brutalism is complete without this ensemble.

Germany versus the USSR

In Montréal rivalry between nations shifted from competition to produce the most innovative and elaborate exhibit to a beauty competition, a contest to create the most exciting pavilion. The Soviet and German pavilions, for instance, competed with one another for the prize for the roof with the longest cantilever.

The Federal Republic of Germany was represented by a pavilion designed by Frei Otto and Rolf Gutbrod. A terraced exhibition area was covered with a tent roof suspended from eight steel masts; the roof consisted of a lattice of steel cables and a polyester skin. This building is regarded

Südwestdeutsches Archiv für Architektur und Ingenieurbau

Key works of German post-war architecture: the expo pavilion by Rolf Gutbrod and Frei Otto (1967); below: view of the expo area during the 1967 world exhibition.

Interior view of the German Pavilion: the lecture hall was subsequently used as a cinema (photo from July 1971).

3

as a precursor for the Olympic Stadium in Munich, which was built shortly afterwards and was, you might say, the same design built on a larger scale. The airy tent gave visitors the opportunity to inspect, among other things, a reproduction of the workplace at which Otto Hahn discovered atomic fission. Also exhibited were optical instruments, a German-made camera with which the US astronauts had photographed in space, the German deep-sea diving device (bathyscaph) with which the Swiss oceanographer Jacques Piccard had undertaken his underwater expeditions, and a replica of the Gutenberg Bible. Later it turned out that the project's US-American leader was a criminal whom the FBI had put on its list of wanted persons …

three levels made it easier to present the very different exhibits of a vast empire which at the time had a population of 230 million. In addition to a Tupolev airplane, visitors could see, for instance, a model of a nuclear reactor. A particular attraction was the Space Hall, the third level, which exhibited the Soviet Union's contribution to research into space. Its centrepiece was the original space capsule in which Yury Gagarin was the first human being to orbit the Earth.

The pavilion attracted more than 13 million visitors and after the end of Expo 67 was dismantled and taken in pieces to Moscow, where it can be seen to this day at the VDNKh (Exhibition of the Attainments of the National Economy), a kind of mini Soviet Union.

Soviet ski jump

Distinguished by an impressively clear, elegant structure in the style of the 1950s, the USSR Pavilion was designed by the Soviet architect Mikhail Posokhin. Two enormous V-shaped columns supported a backward-sloping convex roof with a vast overhang resembling a ski jump. The roof was made of aluminium panels; attached to it was a glass façade articulated by slender steel struts. The interior housed three exhibition levels that were visually linked to one another by overlaps, openings, and galleries. The

Buckminster Fuller's Biosphère

The USA's entry in this race was a biomorphic geodesic dome with a diameter of 76 metres, which had been developed by the then more-than-70-years-old architect Richard Buckminster Fuller in collaboration with the Japanese engineer Shoji Sadao. The breath-taking, visionary 62-metre-high Biosphère – the Russians, though, mockingly called it a 'soap bubble' – was a sensational success for the USA and is to this day one of the city's main sightseeing attractions. It comprises a modular steel structure

Architect Éric Gauthier transformed the Biosphère into an environmental museum in 1992.

R.M. Nunes/iStock

made from prefabricated parts and covered with a honeycomb of acrylic. Small sunshades permit the interior temperature to be controlled, even if their motors did not function perfectly at the time. A 37-metre-long escalator, the longest in the world at the time of its construction, catapulted visitors to the expo upwards, where they could choose between a moon landscape (containing the original Apollo spaceship), a cinema auditorium, and a café. During the world expo, a monorail line passed through the dome. The glittering exterior skin, which in 1967 proved to be porous to water, was destroyed by a fire in 1976, but the unique dome structure exists to this day and has since 1995 housed a museum on the subjects of water and the environment. The escalator, however, has been replaced with elevators. This impressive, seemingly floating dome set the benchmark for future world exhibitions. No expo after 1967 has made do without a dome structure of some kind or other.

50 million visitors

All in all, Expo 67 was the last world exhibition on whose stage the rivalry between the USA and the Soviet Union, the superpowers of the time, was so openly displayed through rival pavilions and exhibits. It additionally had an enormous influence on architecture and urban planning. For Canada, the home country, the world exhibition proved, despite debts of more than 210 million Canadian dollars, a stroke of good fortune. The expo was convincing in the eyes of the rest of the world, and at home it boosted cohesion among the anglophone and francophone populations of what is, in terms of territory, the second-largest country in the world. That it was the 'frogs', Québec's francophile population, who put Canada on the world stage had to be ungrudgingly admitted by the country's anglophones. 'Expo 67 was part of a modern narrative of two nations – Canada and Quebec,' write David Anderson and Viviane Gosselin in their book *Private and Public Memories of Expo 67* (2008).

Half of the total of 50 million visitors to Expo 67 came from Canada itself; 45 %, from the United States. France alone provided 120,000 visitors to the exhibition. Montréal continues to benefit to this day from construction and infrastructural projects undertaken at that time. The islands on which the expo was held are favourite recreational areas for inhabitants of Montréal. In the middle of the 2000s efforts were made to have a further world exhibition take place on the Expo 67 territory in 2017, precisely 50 years after Expo 67. For financial reasons, however, in the end Montréal did not go through with submitting an application.

Heike Maria Johenning

The casino brings together the former expo pavilions of Québec and France.

The concrete monsters of Montréal

Brutalism is a Modernist architectural style which dominated mainly between 1960 and 1980 – and, curiously, on all five continents. It is regarded as a transitional style between Modernism and Postmodernism and as a form of architectural expressionism. Typical features of Brutalism are its emphasis of load-bearing structures, symbiosis of simple geometrical forms, and the coarse manner in which its buildings are designed and presented. Employed mainly for public buildings such as universities, industries, schools, and research institutions, Brutalism created colossal monoliths which are characterised by exaggerated monumentality, great plasticity of façades, and dramatic overhangs.

The designation 'Brutalism' derives from the French term *béton brut* (raw concrete). Raw concrete was promoted as the preferred material in France by Le Corbusier; subsequently, its use spread from Europe to other continents. As a construction material, concrete was easily moulded into the desired shape; it was regarded as 'honest' in view of its rejection of disguising adornment and as attractively low-cost (at a time when although World War II was over, its economic and psychological effects were still very much in evidence). Brutalism was not primarily an aesthetic of raw materials but a new relation between architecture and use, between built structure and spatial practice. Skilful gradations between open and closed volumes allowed Brutalist buildings to merge with their surroundings. Intermediate zones and transitions were spanned using monumental pillars.

There is no purist definition of Brutalism, however; this style cannot be reduced to a single aesthetic. There is no manifesto of Brutalism, nor was there at the time an obligatory construction method. Brutalism was the quest for a new design language; it was a way of providing modern societies with powerful architectures. The rough, repellent surface structures of the concrete façades were intended to refract the light and reinforce the impression of mass and depth. Typical features of this style are scored or bush-hammered façades, ribbed concrete blocks, and the classic 'corduroy look'. The idea of making casting moulds industrially reproducible was innovative. The modular rationality of the prefab construction method was regarded as just as radically modern and progressive as construction using a steel skeleton filled in with glass and concrete blocks. Both were used in Brutalism. The British

3

The British architect Peter Smithson coined the term 'concrete monster'.

architect Peter Smithson, whose reputation spread far beyond the borders of
his home country, was of the view that
Brutalism was 'not about the construction material, but about its qualities and
its impact.'

Caves versus goldfish bowls

In North America, in contrast to European
variants of this highly variable style, the
use of exposed concrete and demon-
strative display of structural elements
were a reaction to monotonous curtain-
wall office buildings and the open-plan
floor plans of bungalows in the suburbs.
In contrast to Le Corbusier, the English
architecture critic Reyner Banham defined the New Brutalism (1953–1966) as
a variant of Brutalism which permitted
the use of other materials too, such as
metal, brick, and stone. At a conference
in 1954 the US architect Paul Rudolph ac-
cused the assembled architects of 'building too many goldfish bowls and too few
caves.' He envisioned 'living, breathing,
dynamic rooms of endless diversity.'
Primarily due to their intimidating scale,
off-putting waywardness, and unusual
materiality, the cavernous concrete
giants found little acceptance among the
general public. In the 1990s the style fell

into disrepute because the exposed-concrete façades aged badly and emanated
an aura of neglect.

#SOSBrutalismus

The beginning of the twenty-first century brought the onset of a phase of re-
discovery given that in the meantime
a significant number of these massive buildings had been demolished, reduced in size, or disfigured. The web-
site www.sosbrutalism.org, launched by
the German Architecture Museum (DAM)
in Frankfurt am Main, the Wüstenrot
Stiftung (Wüstenrot Foundation) and the
digital magazine *uncube* in 2015, func-
tions as an online databank. Currently,
its list comprises 2000 Brutalist buildings from all over the world. The project's
goal is to increase public awareness of
these buildings as monuments in need of
protection, register concrete monsters
threatened with demolition, and classify
them in order of degree of threat.

Next double page:
Colour underground: wall art in the
Montréal metro.

The Montréal metro:
a mirror of visual urban culture

Boris Chukhovich
art and architecture historian, Montréal

If there was a 'Golden Age' in the history of Montréal, then, seen from today's perspective, it was undoubtedly the period of the 'Quiet Revolution' which occurred in the 1960s. In the province of Québec this was an era characterised by the secularisation of society and the creation of the welfare stare. Additionally, education and health, which had until then been dominated by the Roman Catholic Church, were brought under the control of the state. Finally, Montréal, the metropolis of the French-speaking province of Québec, stepped into the international limelight almost overnight with two major events in the 1960s and 1970s: Expo 67 and the Olympic Games of 1976. The international character of these important events brought large numbers of foreign architects to Canada. The largest Modernist project realised by the city of Montréal between 1960 and 1980, however, involved local as opposed to foreign urban planners and artists: the construction of the city's underground railway (metro). It was here that the most important tendencies in Montréal Modernism would ultimately take shape.

Modernist tendencies had been present in the art of Montréal from the 1920s; however, due to the isolation of urban cultural life in the province of Québec and the conservative attitude of the dominant Catholic Church, they for a long time remained marginalised and subordinate to the artistic Avant-garde in Europe and the Soviet Union. The first art movement to articulate the ambitions of Montréalers came into being in the middle of the 1940s and made its voice heard in the manifesto *Le Refus Global* (Total Refusal). The work of the painter Paul-Émile Borduas, the manifesto was signed by 15 authors and artists from various artistic movements. Its subject was the 'crisis of Christian civilisation' and the necessity of submitting to an 'unconditional need for freedom'. The artists put their faith in the principles of 'Les Automatistes': liberation of the subconscious and a shift towards non-figurative art and abstraction. Despite the group's underwhelming success and the emigration of its principal spokesmen, some of the ideas of the 'Automatistes', who promoted intuitive methods in painting and stream of

Métro-Pavillon Champ-de-Mars with 'dancing forms' by the Les Automatistes group of artists.

consciousness as a source of inspiration, were taken up by large numbers of artists. Two of the signatories of *Le Refus Global*, Marcelle Ferron and Jean-Paul Mousseau, played an important role in the design of Montréal's metro.

Art in the metro

The idea of building a metro for Montréal was first suggested at the beginning of the 1910s. The practical realisation of this plan, however, came only in 1961, at the peak of the Quiet Revolution, a period which brought radical modernisation to the province of Québec. The metro's architecture was to make this process visible. At the beginning of construction two strategic decisions were taken. First: each station was to be unique and to be designed by a different architecture firm. Second: Montréal was to be the first western world city after Stockholm whose metro was to be not just a public transport system but also a space for public art. The Montréal metro's originality and current appearance are ultimately the result of fierce debate.

The original design of the metro stations envisaged spaces containing pictures taken from Montréal's history and culture. This is especially true of the underground stations on the first line, which opened in 1966. The Place-des-Arts station featured a backlit stained-glass window by Frédéric Back on the subject of the history of music. Berri-UQAM station has a stained-glass window by Pierre Gaboriau and Pierre Osterath depicting the city's founders. Papineau station has a fresco by Jean Cartier showing the 'Patriote Rebellion', the uprisings against the British Crown in 1837–1838.

The works of art for the metro were financed through donations and were only realised after the money had actually come in. Two stations on the first line received abstract instead of figurative artworks: Peel station (architects: Paineau, Gérin-Lajoie et Leblanc; artists: Jean-Paul Mousseau and Claude Vermette; 1966) and Champs-de-Mars (architect: Adalbert Niklewicz, 1966). Peel station has coloured ceramic discs with stripes in shades of orange and blue (diameter: from 1.8 to 3.6 metres). Of the original

Boris Chukhovich

37 ceramic discs bring colour to the grey of Peel metro station.

48 discs, 31 are still in existence. A vast stained-glass window with hand-blown glass elements decorates the pavilion of Champs-de-Mars station. The spatial composition *Les grandes formes qui dansent* (The large dancing forms) occupies three of the four walls of the distribution level. Marcelle Ferron, the artist who created it, was a member of the Automatistes and had – like Mousseau – signed the *Le Refus Global* manifesto. Both argued that, following completion of the stations, their works of art should be seen not in isolation but as part of the spatial composition of the metro station itself and as radically modern. Ferron described the relation between architecture and art as 'a marriage of love', as opposed to 'an ordinary marriage'. This approach proved groundbreaking. After 1973, works of art were an essential part of every architecture project in Montréal. When estimates of costs were drawn up for metro stations, a fixed part of the budget was from the outset assigned to works of art.

Monochrome colour wheels and coloured stripes

In addition to the 'Automatistes', another Modernist art movement whose aesthetic had a strong influence on the

Boris Chukhovich

The abstract tile patterns in orange and blue are firmly anchored in the city's iconography.

In this stained glass window Frédéric Back tells the story of music in Montréal.

metro stations took shape in Montréal from the middle of the 1950s: the 'Plasticiens' – a group of painters who called for the classical picture composition based on a division into foreground and background to be rejected in favour of more abstraction. While the 'Automatistes' referred to Surrealism and tried to capture the subconscious, the 'Plasticiens' concentrated on plastic resources such as materials, form, and colour. In the 1950s these two experimental groups of artists were still relatively unknown, but in the 1960s their works were already being shown in museums. Their artistic explorations led ultimately to an enrichment of the urban spatial structure in Montréal's metro. An entire series of metro stations were designed by the 'Plasticiens', who specialised in monochrome flecks of colour, concentric circles, and painted metal panels. These included, for instance, Pell, LaSalle (architects: Gillon & Larouche; artists: Peter Gnass and Michèle Tremblay-Gillon; 1978), and Jean-Talon (architects: Duplessis, Labelle, Derome; artists: Gilbert Sauvé and Judith Klein; 1966) stations. Vertical strips of colour by sculptors such as Guido Molinari and Claire Sarrasin are to be found at Villa-Maria (architect: André Léonard; 1981) and Parc (architects: Blouin, Blouin & Associés; 1987) stations. Thus a circle of 'dissident artists' evolved into an influential community of artistic creators who from the 1950s forwards played an active part in designing the urban environment and gave Montréal an absolutely distinctive visual code and a special identity.

Museum of Brutalist masterpieces

The aesthetic of the Montréal metro is additionally characterised by a pronounced preference for Brutalism. While everywhere else in the world Brutalist buildings are currently being demolished because they have failed to withstand the weather or have aged badly, Montréal to this day possesses an entire underground museum of Brutalist masterpieces. Stations in which the focus is on playing with the expressive properties of concrete include Peel, Bonaventure (architect: Victor Prus; 1967), Jolicoeur (architect and artist: Claude Boucher; 1978), Verdun (architect: Jean-Maurice Dubé; artist: Antoine D. Lamarche; 1978), De l'Église, LaSalle (architects: Didier, Gillon et Larouche; 1978), Lionel-Groulx (architect: Yves Roy; 1978), Préfontaine (architect: Henri Brillon; 1976), Pie-IX (architect: Marcel Raby; architect: Jordi Bonet; 1976), Côte-Sainte-Catherine (architect and artist: Gilbert Sauvé; 1982), Angrignon (architect: Jean-Louis Beaulieu; 1978), and De La Savane (architects: Guy de Varennes and Almas Mathieu; artist: Maurice Lemieux; 1984).

Boris Chukhovich

The pavilion at Angrignon station has a roof of semi-cylindrical Plexiglas domes in red frames.

Traditional Brutalism, which is defined by its construction material – *béton brut* (raw concrete) – spawned a further variant, so-called 'brick Brutalism'. This is to be found in the following stations: Snowdon (architect: Jean-Louis Beaulieu; artist: Claude Guité; 1988), Place-Saint-Henri (architects: Julien Hébert and Jean-Louis Lalonde; artists: Jacques de Tonnancour, Julien Hébert, and Joseph-Arthur Vincent; 1980), and Lucien-L'Allier (architects: David, Boulva & Cleve; artist: Jean-Jacques Besner; 1980).

The metro as movie set

Finally, another distinctive feature of the Montréal metro is the theatrical quality of its large entrance areas, where massive, exposed pillars are employed to connect several levels: the entrance, the stairs, and the distributive platforms leading to the individual platforms. Such spaces have usually been created in the form of sequentially arranged volumes that are linked to one another by passages. In Montréal, due to the open method of construction, the underground spaces often have the form of a theatre auditorium in which you can look down on the 'stalls' and the 'stage' from the 'gallery'. Perhaps the most expressive spaces are at the following stations:

Luicien-L'Allier, Place-Saint-Henri, Villa-Maria, Namur (architects: Labelle, Marchand et Geoffroy; artist: Pierre Granche; 1984) and Outremont (architects: Dupuis, Chapuis & Dubuc; artist: Gilbert Poissant; 1988). This ambience has made Montréal's metro a favourite setting for films. Scenes that have been shot here include parts of the thriller *The Jackal* with Bruce Willis and Richard Gere and the drama *Jesus of Montreal* (1989) by the Québec director Denis Arcand, in which the protagonist 'dies' on the 'stage' in front of Place-Saint-Henri station.

Translated from Russian into German by Heike Maria Johenning and from German into English by John Nicolson

Right: the stained glass at Berri-UQAM station pays homage to the city's founders.

From Postmodernism to the present day

A city at the heart of globalisation

From grey to colourful

With the passing of the years the characteristic grey of Montréal's limestone houses has become less dominant: this stone, which is highly valued but difficult to quarry, is now used only for ornamentation. If the city with the largest proportion of stone buildings on the North American continent looks strikingly colourful today, there are a number of reasons why. First, there are the façades of the Victorian buildings, which have recently been repainted. But there is a second factor which helps to give this metropolis, where snow can lie on the ground for sometimes six months at a time, a friendly appearance: the joyfully chromatic, supersized street art.

Historical factory buildings and warehouses are, as in Europe, being converted and/or renovated. What used to be port complexes are likewise undergoing a facelift and are now drawing the public to the water – and this is in a city which has traditionally lived with its back turned to the river.

Multi-ethnic model city

Montréal has evolved into an innovation centre. In the fields of multimedia, biotechnology, software, artificial intelligence, film, and music it now serves as a source of impulses for Europe. Also, Facebook, Google, Samsung, Microsoft, and IBM have incubators here. In 2015 Justin Trudeau was elected prime minister of Canada and moved from Montréal to Ottawa. Valérie Plante, who has been mayor of Montréal since 2017, is the city's first female mayor.

Montréal is Canada's cultural capital and has been a UNESCO City of Design since 2006. A multi-ethnic model city in which two world languages are spoken as official government languages, it is currently experiencing a construction boom. On the one hand, work is being

L'Euphorie des Sages (2008) by Carlito Dalceggio.

Heike Maria Johenning

done on existing buildings; on the other, new glass structures are shooting up into the sky. Sometimes, there is a tendency to forget that the east of Canada is not immune to the onward march of climate change: summers in Montréal are becoming ever warmer.

Southern sun

Boulevard St Laurent has ceased to be a language boundary. For decades it was the case that if you lived east of this street ('à l'Est'), you were francophone, whereas inhabitants of the district west of it ('à l'Ouest') were English-speaking. Some sources even speak of Montréal as a 'divided city'. Paradoxically, this boulevard does not at all divide the city north-south; rather, it runs west-east – creating what is actually an anglophone north and a francophone south. The reason for the confusing uncoupling of street names and more real compass directions is a proclamation of 1792, based on an erroneous assessment of the direction of flow of the Saint Lawrence River. In terms of geography, the river in fact flows from south to north. This was ignored by the city's founding fathers, and Montréal's main axes were named based on a west-east direction of flow. Because the cardinal points were rotated 90 degrees clockwise, on the streets of Montréal the sun rises in the south, not the east.

4

Dan Hanganu designed some notable buildings in Montréal, including Pointe-à-Caillière Museum.

Heike Maria Johenning

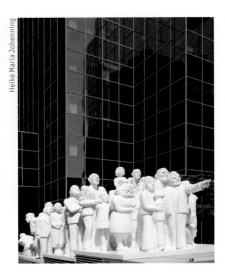

La Tour Richter
1981, av. McGill College
René Menkès of
WZMH Architects
1981

112 C

These two linked glass towers rise in the centre of Montréal like an open book. However, the two 'parts of the book' are of different design. The left structure of the complex, which is clad with reflective glass, is 16 storeys high and has more 'pages'; the right part is 20 storeys high. In contrast with the high-rises with square ground plans that were common in the 1960s, this asymmetrical, flat-roofed building with projections and pointed corners looks like a fanning-out iceberg. Occupied today by Industrielle Alliance, this monolithic office building has been awarded various architecture prizes. In 1986 it was enhanced with the installation of *La Foule Illuminée* (The Illuminated Crowd), a sculpture by the British sculptor Raymond Mason, in front of its entrance. A group of figures made from varnished, beige-coloured polyester resin comprises 65 people of all age groups and ethnicities; their 'leader' points towards a point in the distance. The further back a figure stands in this group, the less illuminated he or she seems to be. Joy and sorrow are reflected in the figures' faces and gestures. Another crowd piece by Raymond Mason, *La Foule* (1968), may be seen in the Tuilerie Gardens in Paris.

Heike Maria Johenning

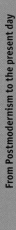

Maison Alcan

1130, rue Sherbrooke Ouest
*ARCOP et Associés; Peter Rose,
Peter Lanken, Julia Gersovitz*
1982

113 C

Postmodernism brought to Montréal a tendency to abstract the elements of previous styles, but it also brought new construction materials. Known as Maison Alcan, the headquarters of the aluminium manufacturer Alcan includes two previously existing buildings in different styles: a villa with a striking circular bay window and corner tower built in 1894, once home to Lord Atholstan, and a red-brick building from 1928, which used to be the Berkeley Hotel. In 1981 Alcan bought the entire street block to accommodate offices for its management. A new building was nevertheless needed in the rear area of the lot.

Its façade consists of set-back volumes with distinctively shimmering aluminium cladding and stands out pleasingly from the surrounding historical buildings and the typical high-rises of the 1980s. The idea of revitalising old buildings in the centre and adapting them for new uses was in its day a milestone in Montréal's urban planning; this project is a good example. In 2015 the firm nevertheless moved into a new building, daunted by the financial expenditure required for renovation of the seven historical structures, of which four are listed architectural monuments. The new owner is Guy Laliberté, the founder of Cirque du Soleil. The artist and entrepreneur, who flew to the International Space Station in 2009, is apparently not frightened by the cost of the mammoth project that revitalising this complex is turning out to be.

Centre Canadien d'Architecture (CCA)

1920, rue Baile
Peter Rose, Phyllis Lambert
1985–1988

114 B

The Canadian Centre for Architecture (CCA) had already been founded when this Postmodernist building was devised in 1979. The architect, curator, and patron Phyllis Lambert worked with Peter Rose on the design for the CCA's building. With a U-shaped ground plan, it was intended to wrap around on two sides the historical Maison Shaughnessy (built: 1875), then threatened with demolition. The two-and-a-half-storey building has an almost entirely undecorated façade of characteristic grey Montréal limestone and a small number of simple windows on its front side. For this reason it at first glance looks rather off-putting. The two wings of this building, which contains a total of 12,000 square metres of floor space, are asymmetrical. One ends in a curved bay window, which seems to take its cue stylistically from the winter garden of Maison Shaughnessy (see: 021). The other likewise culminates in a curved corner. The only façade decoration is a kind of aluminium cornice, which also decorates the curves and seems to coil, high up, around the flat roof. The exhibition spaces inside the building have large skylights which admit abundant daylight into the interior, which is lined with Québec granite, aluminium, and maple. Decades of work by Phyllis Lambert are to thank for the fact that the CCA is today a research institution with an international reputation. The building's spatial programme includes ateliers, editorial offices, an auditorium, a restoration workshop, a restaurant, and a bookshop. Lambert's credo – 'We are not a museum that exhibits works and says, "That is architecture,"; we try to stimulate people to reflect' – remains to this day the CCA's guiding principle and has contributed to this institution becoming known far beyond Canada's borders. Phyllis Lambert (born: 1927) comes from a Jewish industrial family called Bronfman. She worked with Mies van der Rohe on, among other things, the Toronto Dominion Centre. The CCA's archive of pictures and documents is one of the most extensive of its kind in the world, which is why the number of windows on this building had to be limited for security reasons. Parts of the estates of Peter Eisenman, Arthur Erickson, Ernest Cormier, James Stirling, and Frank Lloyd Wright are kept here and may be viewed on site. The CCA possesses a sculpture garden in which Melvin Charney has playfully interpreted the Classical inheritance of occidental architecture: visitors stroll first through fragments of a palace, including an open staircase, before coming suddenly face to face with a mini-Parthenon with concrete pillars.

Philipp Meuser

1250 René-Lévesque
1250, boulevard
René-Lévesque Ouest
Kohn Pedersen Fox Associates
1988–1992

One of the most modern and most beautiful skyscrapers in this city stands on a square plinth on a site formerly occupied by a Presbyterian church. The 47 storeys of this 226-metre-high office building

divide into a number of stacked volumes which develop into a flat high-rise tower with two asymmetrical main façades. The middle part of the convex curtain façade of glass and aluminium is reinforced by a structure consisting of pillars. The second façade, with three set-backs, has granite cladding and plain square windows. The north block, perpendicular to the tower, is a lower structure which steps down to interlock with the lower development on

Philipp Meuser

this side. On the right side of the building an antenna incorporated in the top six storeys projects 30 metres into the sky, emphasising the building's verticality. A trademark of the renowned New York architects KPF is the sunscreen-like 'crown' in place of a cornice – an allusion to the Statue of Liberty in New York. A similar element adorns the high-rise Westendstraße 1 in Frankfurt am Main, likewise by Kohn Pedersen Fox, which was erected in 1990–1993. The much larger steel crown of this building's younger brother in Frankfurt weighs 95 tonnes and can even be heated in the winter. Another distinctive feature of Montréal's tallest skyscraper is an atrium in the fourth storey, which houses a winter garden planted with bamboos.

Nicolas McComber/iStock

1000 De La Gauchetière

116 C

1000, rue de la Gauchetière
Lemay et Associés,
Dimitri Dimakopoulos et Associés
1991–1992

This 51-storey skyscraper rises 205 metres above a square ground plan and has a special place in Montréal's skyline. Like the Empire State Building in New York, it slightly tapers towards the top, has vertical recesses, and possesses a unique triangular pointed roof – only in this case made from copper and without an antenna. In distinction to second-generation skyscrapers from the period around 1900, here the tripartite division into base, shaft, and capital has largely disappeared. With its façade of polished granite, which wraps around the uniformly square windows like a light-coloured grid, this monolith looks almost as if it has been cast in one piece. Its four copper entrance domes are inspired by those of the nearby cathedral. The name of the street, which is also the name of this skyscraper, derives from a French officer called de la Gauchetière, to whom this plot of land once belonged. Today De La Gauchetière with its view of Marie-Reine-du-Monde Cathedral (see: 020) is home to CDPQ (Caisse de dépôt et placement du Québec), the Canadian national pension company. Its podium houses a shopping centre and an artificial skating rink.

4

bakerjarvis/iStock

Pavillon Jean-Noël Desmarais/ 117 C
Musée des Beaux-Arts
1380, rue Sherbrooke Ouest
Moshe Safdie,
Desnoyers Mercure & Associés,
Lemay Leclerc
1991

A team of architects led by Moshe Safdie, who achieved world fame with the thundering success of his Habitat 67 residential complex (see: 102) at Expo 67 in Montréal but has only seldom designed buildings to be erected in Canada, was given the brief of designing an additional pavilion for the Musée des Beaux-Arts (see: 052 and 107) to house its collections of modern and contemporary art. The new building needed to incorporate the adjacent block of historical urban houses and to guide passers-by from the pavement into the museum.

Glass was the ideal construction material for this purpose. Moshe Safdie must be given credit too for the numerous apertures in the façade; these include gables, skylights, large portholes, and windows, bringing light from all directions into the interior of the three volumes, which are linked by bridges. The front façade greets us with a monumental, rectangular portico without columns and a wide, receding slope of glass. This atrium contains the main entrance. The adjacent historical façade, formerly the New Sherbrooke Apartments, has been preserved. This part of the building contains offices for management and a bookshop. Safdie also gave thought to the navigation system: visitors are always brought back to the atrium. This building was controversial from the outset, but the museum has become more popular with each passing year.

Heike Maria Johenning

World Trade Centre Montreal   118 C
747, rue Square-Victoria
ARCOP et Associés, Provencher_Roy
1992

This complex bearing the world-famous name and logo is an outstanding example of successful urban renewal. An entire street block containing several small buildings from the Victorian age, larger buildings such as the Bank of Nova Scotia, and the Édifice Canada Steamship Lines now operates under one roof, so to speak. The realisation of the 116,000-square-metre shopping, office, and hotel complex was made possible by the construction of a glass roof over an old lane, the Ruelle des Fortifications, which the architects converted with great feeling for the historical basis into a ten-storey atrium. The transformative power of this 'horizontal skyscraper', as the architects from the Montréal firm ARCOP call the complex, is scarcely visible from outside because there have been no changes to the original façades. Only a pair of glass fronts have been added. On the other hand, the ensemble has been connected to Montréal's underground city (Ville intérieure). The lane itself is the landing site of a very special piece of jetsam from German history. To mark the anniversary of the city's founding in 1992, the city of Berlin gave Montréal an especially beautifully painted relict of the Berlin Wall.

Philipp Meuser

Musée d'Art Contemporain
185, rue Ste-Catherine Ouest
Jodoin Lamarre Pratte et
Associés, architectes
1992

119 C

Montréal's Musée d'art contemporain (MAC), situated on Place des arts, is an ensemble consisting of three narrow blocks arranged in parallel, each of which has a steep, pointed-gable glass roof clad in copper. The complex houses exhibition rooms, conservation areas, archives, offices for the museum's management, a multi-purpose theatre (Cinquième Salle), an underground multimedia room for 250 visitors, and a media library. Rising up in the centre of the middle section is a copper-clad,

six-storey block which offers additional exhibition spaces. The façade overlooking the Place des arts is of simple white sandstone with floor-to-ceiling windows. There are unmistakable borrowings from Brutalism: the façades are clad with concrete panels, and there are concrete pillars on all sides of the building. The ground floor contains a restaurant; the second storey has recesses but no windows. The museum's centrepiece is the rotunda in the foyer; from here you can reach the exhibition spaces and the café. The open-plan ground plan reveals certain weaknesses of the design: for instance, the staircases are not easy to find at the first go. The MAC building is currently undergoing renovation (Saucier + Perrotte/GLCRM).

Philipp Meuser

Pointe-à-Callière

350, place Royale
*Dan S. Hanganu with
Provencher_Roy*
1990–1992

120 C

Philipp Meuser

On this historic site in the Vieux Port the task was to integrate the three-century-old remains of Montréal's nucleus into a new building for a museum of archaeology to mark the 350th anniversary of the founding of Montréal in 1992, while also creating an underground access to the Old Customs House (see: 007). The exposed location on an intersection and the shape of the plot of land (which resembles a slice of cake) posed particular challenges. Nevertheless this steamship-like, flat-roofed building with stylised chimney, is a veritable landmark ... and a magnet for visitors. It was designed by the renowned architect Dan Hanganu, who had studied in Bucharest and lived in Canada since 1970. He gave his elegant design, which he developed with great feeling for the surroundings, the name 'Éperon' (Prow). The nickname signifies a bowsprit or a ramming prow, a widening of the bow of a warship. Here the 'nose' rises four storeys above the five-storey museum building clad with dressed grey limestone, like a vertical continuation of the curved corner. The façades have relatively few and narrow windows;

some of these, however, have been combined into strips stretching over four storeys. The building's surprising feature is the interior design featuring exposed concrete. The exhibition showcases archaeological finds discovered on site: the foundations of the old canal system and the walls of the city's first Catholic cemetery have been fitted with multi-media installations and walkways; a model of the city can be observed under a glass floor. The area between the museum and the old customs building had to be raised one metre so that visitors could walk upright in the crypt. The museum is named after Louis-Hector de Callière (1648–1703). The then governor of New France lived here in 1695 in a castle-like building. In the nineteenth century the Royal Insurance Company had a more prestigious building erected on this site, but it was destroyed by a fire. Hanganu's corner structure is a clear reminiscence of the tower of the insurance building.

HEC Montréal

3000, chemin de la
Côte-Ste-Catherine
*Dan S. Hanganu/Jodoin Lamarre
Pratte et Associés*
1992–1996

121 D

The headquarters building of the École des hautes études commerciales de Montréal (HEC; see: 049) resembles an ocean liner,

JHVEPhoto/iStock

albeit with no curved corners. This vast ensemble is more than seven storeys high and comprises 45,000 square metres of gross office space. Erected on a rectangular ground plan, but with four different façades, the building has been assembled from several cubes linked by intermediate storeys and metal struts. Enormous metal pipes placed at the main entrance – a reminder of the silos in the Old Port – emphasise the sober industrial look. One of the building's sides is glazed over four storeys and houses an open winter garden; the storeys overhanging the garden seem to be propped up only by slender metal columns. At the centre of this 'ship' a cylindrical volume channelling daylight from the roof all the way to the ground floor forms the centrepiece of this decidedly Postmodernist university building.

4

New architecture in Montréal

Montréal is the only city in Canada designated a 'City of Design' by UNESCO, and there is good reason for this. Multicultural, with a long history of immigration, Montréal has a liveliness of spirit that attracts creative talents from all over the world – especially in the fields of fashion, graphic design, and interior design. Four universities offer specialist studies in design, architecture, and urban planning. Montréalers' non-conformism is also reflected in the city's modern architecture. The dynamic, arts-related architecture scene has in recent years produced a wealth of extravagant and innovative designs. For instance, at the beginning of the new millennium extensions were created for the entertainment firm Cirque du Soleil, including a glass cube for use as an acrobatics arena and a residential complex with artists' workshops. The new CDP bank building – conceived as an acute-angled block with a ten-storey-high atrium – has turned out to be a 'horizontal skyscraper' (see: 124).

Since the beginning of the 2000s the main tendencies have been renovation of existing buildings and a return to the value of historical buildings. For instance, the former Dow Planetarium has been converted into an incubator for technology and innovation (see: 128). Villa Mount Stephen has been connected to a glass skyscraper and is today a luxury hotel with historical charm and state-of-the-art technology (see: 026). A degree of political stability and the city's increasing prosperity have also, however, led to a boom in new construction in the high-end segment in apartments and hotels. The new Four Seasons with its residential tower and the extension of the Ritz-Carlton (see: 050) were the starting signal for a revitalisation of the Golden Square Mile district, home to Canada's anglophone elite in the nineteenth century. The Rio Tinto Alcan Planetarium was built in 2013 in the immediate vicinity of the Olympic Stadium (see: 106).

Some gigantomaniac new construction buildings have also been realised – such as the CHUM megaclinic, which consists of three more-than-60-metre-high towers and three annexes in the middle of Montréal's downtown (see: 127). This hospital complex is the largest of its kind in North America. Another megaproject is the Maestria Condominiums skyscraper with its illuminated connecting bridge at the level of the twenty-sixth and twenty-seventh storeys in the Quartier des Spectacles (see: 130). The

new Insectarium in the Botanical Garden, is, on the contrary, subtle, down-to-earth, and full of grace; this was realised in cooperation with the Berlin architecture firm Kuehn Malvezzi (see: 129).

There are also ideas for the Old Port. A new cruise-ship terminal and a floating public baths are in planning. Valérie Plante, the current mayor of Montréal, has in recent years untiringly campaigned for construction of a modern network of tram lines. The planned pink line (Ligne rose) is to run between Villa Marie and Lachine.

At the edge of the city an entirely new residential area – Royalmount – is currently under construction. This promises to be nothing less than a paradigm shift. The team led by the chief designer, Andrew King of Lemay Architects, initially had to rework their first proposal for the planned new district because it was 'insufficiently green'. The current version specifies green roofs but also vertical gardens, 450,000 trees, shrubs, other plantings, and a rainwater-recovery system. Royalmount is to be a 100% CO_2-neutral, mainly hydro-powered pedestrian city which will be connected to the De La Savanne and Namur metro stations by a bicycle bridge.

The Institut de politiques alternatives de Montréal (Montreal Institute for Alternative Policy; IPAM) was founded under the leadership of the architect and curator Phyllis Lambert and Héritage Montréal, the city's organisation for protection of monuments. The institute advises on issues in the fields of urban planning, development, and cultural heritage. Its interventions are important because the new generation of architects sees architecture as a process rather than as something which is forever. For instance, architectural icons from the Brutalist period are sometimes disfigured or even completely demolished.

The Montréal architect, architecture critic, and artist Melvin Charney (1935–2012) coined the term 'Montreal-ness' to designate the idea that collective space should be given greater importance than individual buildings, be they edifices of grey Montréal stone, brick urban mansions, or glass high-rises. Montréal's architectural identity still lies in its neighbourhoods made up of various *quartiers* (small sub-neighbourhoods) which define the physical and social identity of its inhabitants. And in this respect Montréal is utterly different from other North American cities.

Humaniti, designed by Lemay, is Montréal's first 'smart vertical community'.

Peterson Condominium by NEUF Architectes.

In order to revitalize the Quartier des Spectacles, the entrance was renewed.

The high-rise district next to Gare Windsor with La Tour Deloitte.

4

NCK inc.

Cirque du Soleil
(headquarters)
8400, 2e avenue
Dan S. Hanganu/
FABG Architects
2000/2007

122 E

The international headquarters of Cirque du Soleil, which was founded by Guy Laliberté in 1984 in the Baie-Saint-Paul district of Québec as a variety and street theatre and is now renowned all over the world, is situated in Saint-Michel, a slightly remote district of Montréal. The campus built in open countryside in 1997 comprises buildings for costume manufacture, set construction, choreography, management, training and schooling, and acrobatics. The various structures were with great ingenuity brought together on this spot at different times and then expanded with extensions. The rectangular blocks are linked to one another by staircases and glass corridors; this gives them a light, airy, slightly provisional look, like a real circus. The entrance hall has a large open staircase, above and under which gangways have been installed high up in the air. Behind the mainly grey metal cladding and cool expanses of glass are to be found a colourful array of open and communicative interior spaces. The complex also includes the École Nationale de Cirque, a circus school erected in 2003. This is a glass cube with two eleven-metre-high acrobatics spaces designed by architecture firm Lapointe Magne et associés. Abutting it is a school building with a rectangular floor plan. Steel panels sloping obliquely downwards on the main façade protect against the sun but admit sufficient daylight into the training rooms.

The Canadian Press/Alamy Stock Photo

Palais des Congrès
1001, place Jean-Paul Riopelle
Saia Barbarese Toupouzanov/
Tétrault Parent Languedoc et
associés/Ædifica
1999–2003

123 C

At first sight this is one of those standard glass boxes – albeit with scintillating wild colours on one side – in which congresses are held. In fact, however, the construction of this 19,000-square-metre congress centre, planned as a linking element between the old city centre and Montréal's downtown, proved technologically changing. The mixed-use building containing 65 meeting rooms had to be built over a motorway and a metro station; it also needed to have its own entrance to Montréal's underground city. Additionally, a number of older buildings had to be integrated into the project. The architects created a glass complex with four different façades, each of which is intended to allude to the architecture of surrounding buildings. The most successful is the façade of

coloured glass overlooking place Jean-Paul Riopelle. Especially in the interior, this building emanates a cheerful atmosphere which is reinforced by the works of art in the public passage on the ground floor. Art reflected in the windowpanes includes *Lipstick Forest* by Claude Cormier.

Heike Maria Johenning

Heike Maria Johenning

**Édifice Jacques-Parizeau
(Centre CDP Capital)**
1000, place Jean-Paul Riopelle
*Renée Daoust,
Gauthier Daoust Lestage Inc.*
2000–2003

124 C

The architects Gauthier Daoust Lestage designated their design for the Québec investment bank CDP Capital a 'horizontal skyscraper'. Consisting of three blocks between ten and 13 storeys high and possessing a total floor area of 70,000 square metres of space, this glass office building picked up a number of architecture prizes. The nine-storey-high atrium is a masterpiece of engineering: an acute-angled glass wedge which links the three blocks and allows a clear view up to the top floors. On the other side of the atrium the open mezzanines of the main section are visible. Suspended high up is a 'trading pod', a cube with a floor area of 500 square metres with blind panes of glass, used as a trading platform for the pension fund. The innovative double-skin façade ensures energy efficiency and air circulation, one of the features which has earned this building a gold LEED certificate. The building's light and efficient structure enabled the project to be realised without endangering tunnels carrying the nearby Ville-Marie expressway. Its volumes merge harmoniously with the surrounding neighbourhood. In 2015 the ensemble was named after Jacques Parizeau, the Canadian economist and politician who was instrumental in establishing CDP in the 1960s and was prime minster of Québec in 1994–1996. The value of this light-filled building is enhanced by impressive works of art, including, in the foyer, one of the finest oil paintings by the renowned Québec artist Jean-Paul Riopelle: *La Roue* (1955).

Heike Maria Johenning

Heike Maria Johenning

Heike Maria Johenning

Grande Bibliothèque

125 **B**

475, boul. de Maisonneuve Est
Patkau Architects/Croft-Pelletier/
Menkes Shooner Dagenais
2001–2005

The construction of Montréal's new 'large' public library at a cost of 100 million CAD was a project of almost gigantic dimensions. Design work on this five-storey building opposite the Université du Québec à Montréal (UQAM) was led by Patkau Architects from Vancouver. A total of 6300 green-shimmering, U-shaped glass plates were fastened to copper uprights to clad the façades of this block-shaped building, which slightly tapers along rue Berri, where its second entrance is situated. The recessed main entrance is signposted by a single load-bearing white column, behind which is a front of windows and an elongated atrium with further columns in a light pink colour. These columns create space for a light-flooded foyer. On the left side are open-plan storeys lined with slats of birch wood (the spaces here are known as *chambres de bois*, a reference to Anne Hébert's novel of the same name). The top fully glazed storey of this flat-roofed building, which contains 33,000 square metres of space and more than four million items, is accessed by an elevator with a panoramic view. The main materials employed in the interior design are wood and aluminium. The Grande Bibliothèque also houses the former National Archive of Québec. The library opened on 23 April (World Book and Copyright Day) 2005. That same year, the city of Montréal was awarded the honorary title 'World Book Capital'.

Planétarium Rio Tinto Alcan
4801, av. Pierre-de Coubertin
Cardin + Ramirez Julien et
Associés, Ædifica
2013

Montréal's new planetarium is situated in the 'Espace pour la vie' museum district beside the Olympic Stadium (see: 106). This part of town also includes cultural buildings with a focus on nature, such as the Biodôme (see: 108) and the Insectarium (see: 129). Two concrete cylinders (diameter: 18 metres) clad with a total of 500 aluminium panels made by the Canadian aluminium manufacturer Alcan each house a vast cinema auditorium (called Chaos and Milky Way). The projector projects 300,000 stars onto the roof of the dome. The Dow Planetarium (see: 128), erected in 1966, managed only 9000; it closed its doors in 2011. The plinth storey contains an exhibition area, a café, and the Exo-World, which examines the possibility of life on other planets (exo-biology). The artistic management was by Michel Lemieux and Victor Pilon. The US firms Sky-Skan and XYZ supplied the multimedia know-how and also created the VR show. This complex of buildings has a platinum LEED certificate.

Philipp Meuser

Heike Maria Johenning

4

Heike Maria Johenning

CHUM
1051, rue Sanguinet;
1000, rue Saint-Denis
*Jodoin Lamarre Pratte
architectes/Menkès Shooner
Dagenais LeTourneux architectes/
Cannon Design + NEUF architectes*
2011–2022

127 C

One of the most modern hospital ensembles in the world, the Centre Hospitalier de l'Université de Montréal (University of Montreal Health Centre, CHUM), was built in several phases over the course of a decade in the middle of the hustle and bustle of the big city. A grand project, the urban-development programme for this site between Montréal's old city centre and downtown included the demolition of the Hôpital Saint-Luc, which was still in use at the beginning of the construction programme. Two other clinics – Hôtel-Dieu de Montréal and Hôpital Notre-Dame – were consolidated to form what is at the present time the largest hospital in North America. The tower of Saint-Sauveur, a church built in 1865, was preserved in response to numerous initiatives by citizens; a part of the church nave was incorporated in the new complex and was enveloped in a glass block, which serves as the entrance. Encompassing 334,000 square metres of gross floor space, CHUM serves as the training hospital of the Université de Montréal and has approximately 1200 rooms for patients. Its four 21-storey high-rises, linked partly by bridges and partly by underground passages, are flanked by the Amphithéâtre Pierre-Péladeau, a multifunctional building whose curved self-supporting exterior skin made from perforated, semi-opaque, copper plates contrasts with the angular volumes of the rest of the CHUM complex and simultaneously forms its centrepiece. The hospital ensemble has six publicly accessible roof gardens and a garage.

Nicolas McComber/iStock

Planétarium Dow
(Centech Incubateur)
1000, rue de la Cathédrale,
Chaboillez Square (Griffintown)
David-Barott-Boulva/MenKès Shooner
Dagenais Le Tourneux Architects
1966/2018

128 **C**

You first have to come up with the idea: a 45-year-old planetarium erected for Expo 67 by the Dow brewery in the middle of Montréal's hip Griffintown district was from 2011 forwards converted into an incubator geared to the generation of radical innovations. This is a place devoted to the creation of synergies between the university and the world of business. The planetarium building belongs to the city of Montréal and now houses a thinktank established by the École de technologie supérieure (ETS). A central circular block rises on a square plinth storey. The building's original design language has been preserved; it conveys movement and enlightenment. Vertical slats and extra-large spotlights form gearwheels symbolising mechanical rotation. The central block is an open circular space housing two large open staircases leading to the storey containing the dome. The glazed office spaces next to the staircase entrances lead to an extensive corridor area which provides access to further offices. The biggest challenge here was to bring sufficient light into the originally dark interior of the building. This was achieved by the employment of a sophisticated lighting concept. The white marble original dome is still used as a screen onto which stars and other celestial objects are projected.

Philipp Meuser

Philipp Meuser

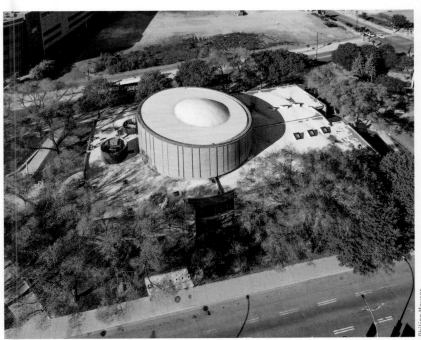

Philipp Meuser

Insectarium du Jardin Botanique

4581, rue Sherbrooke Est
Kuehn Malvezzi,
Pelletier de Fontenay,
Jodoin Lamarre Pratte
2019–2022

129 E

Originally built in the 1990s, the Insectarium was fundamentally redesigned and reconceived from 2019 forwards. It reopened in 2022. A glass quarter-pyramid offers a precisely choreographed and dramatic route through various perception spaces, leading visitors ultimately down to the Earth and then to the habitat of insects. The building envelope with its fan-shaped roof made from wood and glass has a permeability which draws exterior space into the visitor route and thus unites architecture, the museum experience, and landscape. Variations in relations between exterior and interior are addressed in a rich diversity of situations. The architecture goes hand in hand with the landscape, forming a coherent whole. And it likewise meshes with the processes which take place inside it and which take their specific form from outside. For instance, the ridged texture of the roof is based on a leaf pattern. The dome structure containing butterfly cases is clad in an earthy brown.

Maestria Condominiums
300, rue Ste-Catherine Ouest
Lemay Architects
2019–2023/2024

Montréal's Twin Towers, linked by a glass bridge at the 26th and 27th storeys, are destined to become the new landmark on the place des Festivals in the Quartier des Spectacles cultural district.

When completed, they will be Canada's two tallest twin buildings, their silhouettes seeming to touch one another like two dancers. The slender, asymmetrical towers, 194 and 198 metres high, are intended to embody transparency and liveliness. A total of 1750 luxury apartments will offer spectacular views. The towers will also house communal areas and commercial spaces.

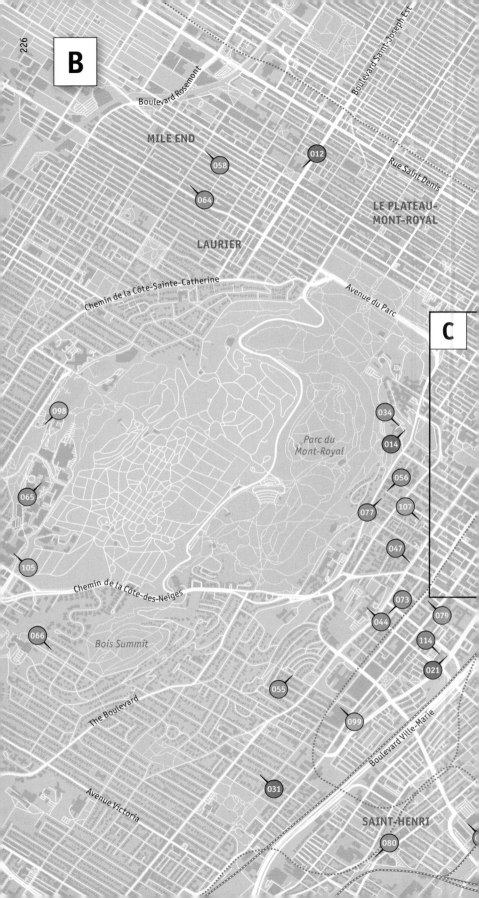

B

Boulevard Rosemont

MILE END

058

012

Rue Saint-Denis

064

LE PLATEAU-
MONT-ROYAL

LAURIER

Chemin de la Côte-Sainte-Catherine

Avenue du Parc

C

098

Parc du
Mont-Royal

034

014

065

056

077

107

047

105

Chemin de la Côte-des-Neiges

073

079

066

044

Bois Summit

114

021

055

The Boulevard

099

Boulevard Ville-Marie

031

Avenue Victoria

SAINT-HENRI

080

Parc
Fontaine

Rue Sherbrooke Est

Avenue De Lorimier

Boulevard René-Lévesque Est

Pont
Jacques-Cartier

Île Sainte-Hélène

Parc Jean-
Drapeau

Fleuve Saint-Laurent

VILLE-MARIE

Gare Centrale

081

068

039

0

125

028

088

025

078

049

062

111

102

0   500 m

D

NOUVEAU-BORDEAUX

Parc Marcelin-Wilson

Autoroute des Laurentides

Avenue O'Brien

Boulevard Marcel-Laurin

Parc Marcel-Laurin

SAINT-LAURENT

Boulevard Alexis-Nihon

017

Autoroute Félix-Leclerc

061

Boulevard Saint-Laurent

Route Transcanadienne

Parc Jarry

082

Boulevard de l'Acadie

Chemin Rockland

Route Transcanadienne

MONT-ROYAL

Chemin Lucerne

121

Chemin de la Côte-des-Neiges

087

Autoroute Décarie

0   500 m

E

SAINT-LÉONARD

Boulevard Viau

Boulevard Lacordaire

089

Route Transcanadienne

NOUVEAU-ROSEMONT

Boulevard Pie-IX

122

Boulevard Saint-Michel

Boulevard Rosemont

ROSEMONT-
LA PETITE-PATRIE

084

Boulevard Saint-Joseph

ANJOU

Parc Félix Leclerc

Boulevard Langelier

Boulevard Rosemont

109

Jardin botanique
de Montréal

129

126

108

106

086

MAISONNEUVE

059

060

Boulevard Pie-IX

HOCHELAGA

Fleuve
Saint-Laurent

0   500 m

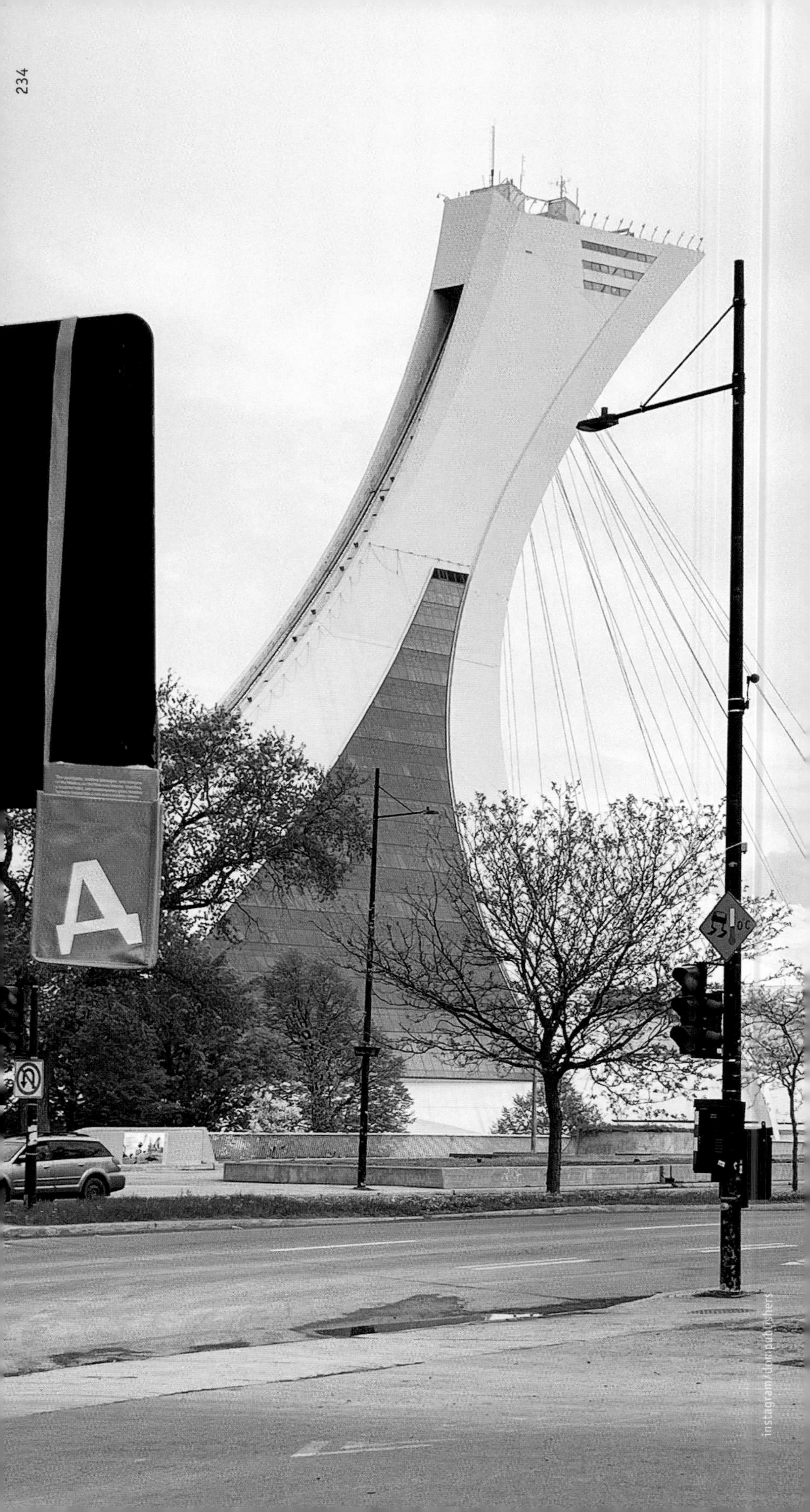
A

Literature

Cohen-Rose, Sandra, *Northern Deco. Art Deco Architecture in Montreal* (Quebec, 1996)

Dagenais, Michèle, *Montreal. City of Water. An Environmental History* (Vancouver, 2017)

Dunton, Nancy/Malkin, Helen, *A Guidebook to Contemporary Architecture in Montreal* (Vancouver, 2008)

Elser, Oliver/Kurz, Philip/Schmal, Peter Cachola (ed.), *SOS Brutalismus: Eine internationale Bestandsaufnahme* (Zürich, 2017)

Johenning, Heike Maria, *CityTrip Montréal* (Bielefeld, 2018)

Kleinmanns, Joachim, *Der deutsche Pavillon der Expo 67 in Montreal. Ein Schlüsselwerk deutscher Nachkriegsarchitektur* (Berlin, 2020)

Korobina, Irina/Rappaport, Alexandr, *Pavilony SSSR na mezhdunarodnykh vystavkakh* (Moscow, 2013)

Linteau, Paul-André, *The History of Montreal. The Story of a Great North American City* (Montreal, 2013)

Linteau, Paul-André/Jaumain, Serge, *Vivre en ville: Bruxelles et Montréal aux XIXe et XXe siècles* (Berne-Bruxelles, 2006)

Lownsbrough, John, *The Best Place to Be – Expo 67 and Its Time* (London, 2012)

Marsan, Jean-Claude, *Montréal en évolution* (Montréal, 1994)

Rémillard, François/Merrett Brian, *Montreal Architecture. A Guide to Styles and Buildings* (Québec, 2007)

Saul, John Ralston, *Reflections of a Siamese Twin* (Toronto, 1997)

Simon, Sherry, *Translating Montréal. Episodes in the Life of a Divided City* (Montreal, 2006)

Vervoort, Patricia, '"Towers of Silence". The Rise and Fall of the Grain Elevator as a Canadian Symbol', *Histoire sociale/Social History 39, 77 (2006)*, pp. 181–204

Ware, Steven, *Montreal* (London, 2001)

Buildings and projects

in order of project number

Seen while making this book

Author

Heike Maria Johenning

Born 1968. Studied Slavic and Romance languages in Munich, Moscow, and Paris. Graduated from SDI München. Since 1996 has worked as a freelance translator and author. Internship with Texpertise Inc. in Montréal. Author of various publications for *Reise Know-How Verlag* and for *DOM publishers* (architectural guides on St Petersburg, Kiev, Tblisi, and Baku).

Left page (clockwise):
Tower of Songs, street-art painting commemorating Leonard Cohen by Gene Pendon and El Mac;
Centre Canadien d'Architecture (see: 114);
ubiquitous in Montréal: the Cirque du Soleil;
Crew Collective, café in the former Royal Bank (see: 071).

The Deutsche Nationalbibliothek lists
this publication in the
Deutsche Nationalbibliografie; detailed
bibliographic data are
available online at http://dnb.d-nb.de.

ISBN 978-3-86922-872-3

© 2023 by DOM publishers, Berlin
www.dom-publishers.com

Proofreading
Uta Keil

Translation from German
John Nicolson

Design
Martina Filippi

QR Codes
Anke Tiggemann

Maps
Ee (Ariel) Dong Chen

Printing
Tiger Printing (Hong Kong) Co., Ltd.
www.tigerprinting.hk